More Praise for SOUL CRAVING

Joel is a student of the soul and a gentle companion on the Way of Jesus. *Soul Craving* can help anyone know and love God more deeply.

—John Ortberg, teaching pastor, Menlo Park Presbyterian Church;
author of *The Life You've Always Wanted*

Joel Warne carefully and skillfully explores the various dimensions of feasting with God and provides rich and clear counsel to those who desire to progress further along the Way.

—Kenneth Boa, president, Reflections Ministries;
author of *Conformed to His Image*

Joel leads the reader on a ruthlessly honest personal journey, revealing his own struggles over the intimacy with Jesus his heart wants most and the undermining pressures and temptations along the way. This books sets before us the joys of a closer walk with God and stimulates us to seek practical realization of God's promise in Leviticus 26:11, 12: "I will put my dwelling place among you. . . . I will walk among you and be your God."

—Jim Raymo, WEC International

Soul Craving is a compelling invitation to intimacy with God. It lifts us above "trying" into transformation.

—Evan B. Howard, author of *Praying the Scriptures*

The themes of *Soul Craving* aim for the heart.

—Jean Leih, spiritual formation pastor,
Westwood Community Church, Excelsior, Minnesota

SOUL
CRAVING

JOEL WARNE

SOUL CRAVING

~ AN INVITATION TO THE FEAST THAT SATISFIES ~

Standard®
PUBLISHING
Bringing The Word to Life

Cincinnati, Ohio

Published by Standard Publishing, Cincinnati, Ohio
www.standardpub.com

© 2002, 2003, 2007 by Joel Warne

Also available: *Soul Craving Group Member Discussion Guide*
978-0-7847-1993-0

Printed in USA.

Visit the author's website, www.WellspringLifeResources.com

Cover and interior design: Mattson Creative
Editor: Diane Stortz

Produced in association with Patti M. Hummel, The Benchmark Group, Nashville, Tennessee.

978-0-7847-1955-8

Library of Congress Cataloging-in-Publication Data

Warne, Joel, 1956-
  Soul craving: an invitation to the feast that satisfies / Joel Warne.
    p. cm.
  Includes bibliographical references.
  ISBN 0-7847-1955-1 (perfect bound)
  1. Spirituality. 2. Spiritual formation. I. Title.

BV4501.3.W362 2007
248.4—dc22
                                      2006024815

13 12 11 10 09 08 07   9 8 7 6 5 4 3 2 1

To Gerri, my treasured companion at the feast

Contents

Hungry

1 The Feast Begins   15
2 Desire   26
3 Already, Not Yet   33

Savoring His Words

4 Liberty   47
5 Encounter   56
6 Unstuck   68

The Flavor of Intimacy

7 Transparency   81
8 Listening   97
9 Worship   113

Relishing His Purpose

10 Purpose   133
11 Calling   149
12 Self-Discovery   172

Satisfied

13 Transformation   189
14 Surrender   203
15 Suffering   217
16 Rest   238
17 Responsiveness   260

Notes   281
Study Guides   285

Taste and see that the LORD is good.
Psalm 34:8

HUNGRY

Jesus declared, "I am the bread of life. He who comes to me will never go hungry."

John 6:35

1 THE FEAST BEGINS

A wintry night some years ago found me in a snug living room with friends, discussing the costs and rewards connected to our journey with God. We had been exploring the Gospel of Luke and had come upon the account of the ill woman who pressed through the crowd to touch Jesus for healing.

The conversation revolved around the risks this woman took in coming to Christ. We noted, for example, that she risked having her request rejected by Jesus, which in a real sense would have felt like a rejection of herself. She also risked being disappointed by Jesus if, for some reason, even if he had wanted to, he had not been able to give her what she desired. And she risked revealing her private, even embarrassing problem to everyone present. Yet, despite the obstacles, she pushed her frail body through the crush of people that surrounded him and drew close to Christ, stretching out a trembling hand to touch him. Luke tells us she received what she sought (see Luke 8:43-48).

We pondered the passage for a while, mulling over its implications for us. What would it mean to touch Jesus Christ as the woman did? What risks might be involved? What difficulties might we face? What would be the rewards? What healing, inner expansiveness, and life answers would it yield? And what might be the costs?

As we kicked these things around, suddenly a voice in the group announced, "You know, I don't think I want to be that kind of Christian." A young man, a regular to the group, continued: "That sounds like a lot of work. I think I would rather just be the sort of Christian, you know, who trusts Jesus for my salvation so when I die I can go to Heaven. But as for all that other stuff—that's too extreme for me."

For an awkward moment or two, the group tried to weigh whether our friend was joking. It turned out he was entirely serious.

The idea of weaving God into one's life in such a way that his companionship flavors every area was apparently not what our friend had signed up for. A safer, less troublesome approach to God was quite enough for him. He preferred a sort of transactional relationship—one in which he would give God just enough trust to get himself just enough salvation to be sure everything worked out safely in the end. But beyond that, he and God would strictly respect each other's space.

Our friend was not new to spiritual things. Of the dozen or so people in the study group, he was the most faithful attendee. He enjoyed the group and it meant a lot to him. But spiritual things were important to him like exercise is important to some people, or gardening, or art. God represented a certain slice of meaning and value in his life. Yet, although you may love to garden, you don't bring your rake and hoe with you everywhere you go, and in his view neither was it practical to bring God into every area of life. Better to simply give him a respected place among many other interests.

I remember feeling a certain pleasure at his honesty. This young man was simply voicing how, as a practical matter, most of us quietly live our lives with God anyway. There are certain "religious" rooms in our hearts in which God is welcome and others into which it doesn't even enter our minds to invite him.

Even though his candor was refreshing, my friend's view was also deflating. I thought, *No, I've got enough disconnected pieces of life to juggle already. I don't need another separate piece called religion to try to balance among them. Instead I need an integrating faith, one that infuses all the individual pieces of my life with a unifying spirit, tone, and direction. A faith that is the focus and springboard of my life. I need an experience of God that speaks to my fractured soul, like Jesus spoke to the ill woman, "Your faith has healed you. Go in peace" (Luke 8:48).*

A permeating relationship like that is certainly what God has in mind. Yet, at first glance, such an integrated, thoroughgoing faith can appear pretty intimidating. You see, to many of us, Christianity largely means a long list of behaviors to achieve, beliefs to maintain, and religious functions at which to put in regular appearances. If that is our experience of faith, then my friend's strategy of isolating his faith to limited and manageable areas of life is a very good plan. After all, aren't our plates terribly full already? Who needs more chores to perform than absolutely necessary?

SOUL CRAVING

I am a pretty good example of the religious-duties-as-faith approach to God. Growing up, I somehow picked up the idea that although God loved me, he didn't like me very much. He loved me because he was God. It was his job to love me. But to get him to like me required that I perform for him at a constantly high level. That sort of relationship with God—one of endless vigilance to keep our accounts current through correct behavior, right thinking, and religious work—deserves to be shrunk to as narrow a sliver of life as possible. There is no water down that well.

18

But what if faith is something different? What if faith means a transforming relationship with someone who consistently breathes life and meaning into everything he touches? What if faith is a heart-to-heart relationship with someone who knows me deeply, accepts me totally, and has the power to increasingly restore my fragmented soul? What if faith opens a doorway into the personal reality every human soul has craved since the day we were born? That would be the sort of faith you would not want to limit, isolate, or confine to out-of-the-way areas of life. Instead, you would want that faith to overflow the few narrow streams of your heart through which it currently trickles until it floods your whole being.

Such a permeating intimacy with God is the goal of this book. An intimate, integrated faith involves:

• weaving the Spirit of Christ throughout all of our daily experience;

• progressively "living into" a new order of things as represented by the cross and resurrection of Jesus Christ;

• steadily escaping a life of cramped self-focus in favor of the expansive things God has planned for us in Christ;

• an inner posture that encourages us to lie intimately upon Jesus' breast until we find our hearts beating more and more in harmony with his.

Such intimacy with God is the treasure in the field that Jesus says is worth selling everything in order to purchase (Matthew 13:44). It's what King David panted after (Psalm 63) and what the apostle Peter flung himself into a sea to pursue (John 21:1–13). It's a bottomless well that slakes your thirst while strangely making you thirstier, a waterfall that washes away the debris of an old life as it irrigates a new life inside.

And the greatest thing of all, from a human perspective, is that such a life is anchored in a relationship of the heart. Transforming intimacy with God is not primarily the product of a set of disciplines (though discipline is involved). It isn't dependent on a grasp of special spiritual insights (though insights are sometimes given). It is not a reward for right behavior, religious productivity, or airy spiritual thinking. Instead, as a relationship of love, it thrives on the kinds of behaviors *lovers* show one another.

BELOVED OF CHRIST

In searching out the attitudes and activities that lead to intimacy with God, it is helpful to ponder intimacy between lovers.

What do lovers want?

How do lovers act?

What do lovers feel?

How do lovers treat one another?

God intends the love demonstrated between human lovers to paint a picture of how intimacy develops between Christ and our souls. Consider these love poems from the Bible's Song of Songs. They illustrate the level of romance God yearns for in our relationship with him:

The King: "Arise, my darling, my beautiful one, and come with me" (Song of Songs 2:10).

The Maiden: "How handsome you are, my lover! . . . Like an apple tree among the trees of the forest is my lover among the young men. I delight to sit in his shade, and his fruit is sweet to my taste" (1:16; 2:3).

The King: "You have stolen my heart, my sister, my bride; you have stolen my heart with one glance of your eyes, with one jewel of your necklace" (4:9).

The Maiden: "My lover is radiant and ruddy, outstanding among ten thousand. . . . His mouth is sweetness itself; he is altogether lovely. . . . I belong to my lover, and his desire is for me" (5:10, 16; 7:10).

Wow! When was the last time your soul swam waters like that with God? There is healing in such intimacy. Power. Deep resources for moving ahead on the journey. And all of this results, not from believing with precise correctness or behaving just right, but from savoring God as your most intimate lover.

Some of us are without romantic mates in this life, either by choice or against our desire. Some of us are married or hope to be one day. Still others of us have met with bitter disappointments in our relationships. Regardless of our experience of human love, God has built inside us, both male and female, a desire for affection and romance that finds its most complete satisfaction in him. "As a bridegroom rejoices over his bride, so will your God rejoice over you" (Isaiah 62:5).

A thousand years from now, all that seems pressing and important today will have been sifted by eternity, leaving us only one great reality to live—the reality of our relationship with God as his prized eternal spouse (Revelation 21). Astounding! This, in the end, says the Bible, is who we are at our most fundamental level—the wedded bride of Jesus Christ. We have no rich dowry to offer, no prestigious family to recommend us, and in case you haven't noticed, our hearts are not all that attractive. Still, not only does God save us, he marries us! What does such a relationship reveal about how God treasures us, about our value to him? What confidence should it lend us about his commitment to provide for and protect us? And how might such security in Christ embolden us to risk the adventures to which he calls us today?

Should we not begin to live the reality of our future intimacy with Jesus Christ right now, in time and space? Should we not make our decisions, approach our difficulties, and live our relationship with our bridegroom out of our identity as his beloved?

Christians have been given a tremendous privilege. First, Christian faith is designed to invade every area of life, including the most ordinary. It is intended to give life a unity, direction, and cohesion, a transforming spirit that seasons one's whole life with the flavor of Heaven. And wonderfully, this faith is not a discipline, a philosophy, or even a religion but a love affair. It commences and grows increasingly vibrant as the lovers daily look into each other's eyes and say "Yes!"

YOUR PLACE AT THE FEAST

It sometimes happens that although we may wish for a more loving, intimate relationship with God, we feel, in fact, distant from him. He is more like a concept or religious idea than a Father or friend. How do we stir love for God? How do we increase our sense of passion for him?

Well, to begin, it might encourage you to realize that by choosing to read a book like this, you are demonstrating a level of passion for Christ already. This same passion, however small, simply needs to be tended and kindled until it burns brighter and brighter. And this can be accomplished in several key ways.

First, simply ask God to deepen your heart's desire for Jesus. It was a happy day in my life when I came across these liberating words in one of the apostle Paul's letters: God is "at work in you, both to will and to work for His good pleasure" (Philippians 2:13, *NASB*). At a time when I thought it was up to me to generate a vibrant love and desire for God, Paul seemed to be saying that this was God's job. Here was a new thought— that if I requested, God would actually form inside me a deeper passion for Christ, a longing for him and his world.

So I asked him to do just that. I prayed something like, "Lord, part of me wants you and part of me doesn't. I can't make myself want you more. I've tried and it doesn't last. Would you please begin to replace my desire for other things with a greater desire for you?"

And he did. Not entirely and not immediately. But over time I noticed a deeper drawing toward God and a delight in things having to do with him that I hadn't known before. I've prayed that prayer many times over the years, and God has always answered it, deepening my love and cementing my passion for him.

Next, as you regularly ask God to increase your appetite for Christ, you will notice a growing taste for things having to do with him. The Bible will seem a little more attractive. Prayer will have greater appeal. You'll feel a heightened hunger to detach from old securities and live with increasing dependence upon God.

Listen to your new appetites! Feed your growing hunger for God with the spiritual food and drink described in the following chapters. This food represents a feast for the soul.

At this feast we take our place at the table alongside the courageous woman of Luke's Gospel. With her, we stretch out uncertain hands to receive from Jesus that peculiar touch that heals our wounds, settles our fears, and forms a filling new wholeness deep inside.

Jesus, my fragmented heart feels a hunger for something I can't describe that I don't find in the world around me. I've tasted a thousand options, and still my longing is sharp. I'm hungry for a home, a place where I'm treasured, an embrace where I am safe and wanted. Could this home be you, dear Jesus? Do your arms hold a place for me? Increase my courage, Lord, to turn day to day from things that leave me empty to feed my heart instead with more and more of you.

Amen.

2 DESIRE

In the end we choose the thing we want the most.

Desire. Desire is a volcanic power. We may say and think that we live by our beliefs, but at the end of the day, our longings shape our decisions more deeply than the things we believe to be true.

As we begin to probe the attitudes and activities that shape our lives in God, we start by pondering the question of inner yearnings. Our desires are terribly important to our quest for God, yet they are not always plain. They are often obscured by a stormy surface restlessness that draws attention to itself, disguising our deeper needs.

The other day, for example, my wife and I were driving home from a visit with our daughter and grandson. It was our day off, still early, and we wondered aloud what we wanted to do next. We both felt like going home, but we noticed we were near a movie theater showing a film we had mild interest in seeing.

The next thing I knew, somebody twelve feet tall had picked me up by one leg, turned me upside down, and was shaking me around until my brain was scrambled. Well, maybe not literally, but that was the feeling I had as I found myself in the theater watching the oversized characters on-screen portray a story designed, it turned out, to agitate and disorient viewers like me.

As the film careened this way and that and pinched and poked me with its ungentle humor, I wondered, *How did I get here? It's a beautiful day outside. Now I get to carry these dreadful images around with me for the next few hours (or days) until they wash away like the debris of some shipwreck.* Deep down I knew this movie was going to be like this and didn't really want to see it that much anyway. Yet it felt like a more exciting option than going home.

Detour

That's how it goes with me sometimes. It seems I have a restlessness inside that wants to be <u>entertained</u>, <u>kept</u> busy and <u>distracted</u>. And I've noticed that this restlessness sometimes encourages me to make choices against my better judgment. Perhaps you've experienced this too. Many find that a sense of unsettledness, a *dis*-ease with life, is a human fact that calls loudly for attention.

I may, for example, be at home, leisurely reading my newspaper, and a half hour later find myself roaming the aisles of a department store hunting for an item I don't really need simply because it winked at me from the corner of an advertisement. It is not the item itself I really want, of course, but a fix for my restlessness habit. The quick trip to the store scratches an itch. It fulfills a temporary need for purpose and provides something to do—a diverting activity to dull my anxieties or stimulate my senses.

Have you ever noticed that a great number of the activities that make up our lives are not chosen because we particularly believe in them or feel God has called us to them? Instead they result from a quest to medicate restless yearnings and appetites. The appetites themselves are often laced with important human needs for purpose and fulfillment, but our solutions to these needs often take us to empty wells. "My people . . . have forsaken me, the spring of living water, and have dug their own cisterns, broken cisterns that cannot hold water" (Jeremiah 2:13).

Sometimes, imperceptibly, bit by bit, the whole arc of our lives can develop into a detour, diverting us from real solutions for our inner needs. Not aware of the true nature of our hunger, we react to surface pricks and pangs in an attempt to find relief.

Excessive work, endless home projects, obsessive hobbies, too much sleep, unwise relationships, or other diversions can become God-substitutes, unintended "empty wells," obscuring authentic answers to our deep human longings.

LISTEN TO YOUR LONGINGS

Some religions deal with the question of human longings by creating spiritual exercises to help people be rid of them. The idea of these religions is that inner desires are inherently bad—they distract us from the deeper issues of life, lead us to poor choices, and set us up for painful disappointments when they are not fulfilled. So the best solution is simply to eliminate them.

Christianity understands inner longings differently. It encourages us to acknowledge our yearnings as given by God. Longings are a central part of what it means to be human.

As a human being, I desire happiness, fulfillment, acceptance, and purpose. I yearn for adventure, romance, mystery, and love. I want meaningful work, companionship, security, and inner rest. These are core human hungers, and there are many others. They are not to be denied or disregarded. They are not to be eliminated or labeled sinful.

In the same way that a feeling of physical hunger reminds me it is time to eat, inner hungers remind me that my heart is looking for nourishment. Longing, pain, anxieties, and other insistent and nameless yearnings are all signals that my soul craves to be fed. The challenge, in a world in which we are surrounded by junk food for the soul, is to cultivate a habit of feeding upon Jesus Christ, the heavenly banquet.

> Come, all you who are thirsty,
>> come to the waters;
> and you who have no money,
>> come, buy and eat!
> Come, buy wine and milk
>> without money and without cost.
> Why spend money on what is not bread,
>> and your labor on what does not satisfy?
> Listen, listen to me, and eat what is good,
>> and your soul will delight in the richest of fare.
>>> —Isaiah 55:1, 2

It's good to listen to our longings. They should be acknowledged and valued. Our longings are springboards from which we can dive into an ever-deeper intimacy with God.

• Am I lonely? I am made for my own love story with God (Hosea 2:14-23).

• Am I bored? My heart was created for adventure in Christ (John 10:10; Hebrews 11:8).

· Am I exhausted from the constant heave-ho of the world in which I live? There is liberal rest in God to seep down to the roots of my soul (Hebrews 4:9, 10).

Am I burned out, disillusioned with my life goals? I was made for deeply valuable purposes in Christ (Matthew 5:14-16; Ephesians 2:10).

In a very real way, inner restlessness is a gift from God. The key to benefiting from restlessness is in asking whether it perhaps springs from deep human needs craving to find nourishment in God. When we try to salve our restlessness independent of God, it leads to a continual experience of disconnection and struggle, competition with God and others, and a hovering sense of having missed the real food of life.

On the other hand, as we become aware of personal inner hungers, we can invite God to draw our longings away from empty wells toward real food and drink in Christ. The more we sample this inner feast, the more it feeds the deep desires that lie beneath our surface agitations, shrinking those fidgety pangs and making them less and less disturbing. When the soul houses a nourishing guest, the restless heart becomes content at home. The coming chapters help us notice where this nourishment lies and how to turn our appetites to that table.

Father, thank you for my longings and even my troubling restlessness. Thank you also for the deep empty places in my soul. I realize now that these are your gifts to me. They refuse the substitute foods with which I have tried to quiet them for so long. Let them lead me to that table where famished people find food fit for their hunger. Let them nudge and prod and guide me until they lead me to my heart's only satisfaction—you, my Father, only you.

Amen.

3 ALREADY, NOT YET

Not long ago I attended a retreat. Among those present was Andy, in his early twenties, who grew up in the church I attend.

Over the course of the two-day retreat, I had a chance to observe Andy as he interacted with the rest of us during group sessions, mealtimes, and other activities. He showed a focus, spiritual wisdom, modesty, and courage that were wonderfully uplifting. As the retreat progressed, I developed a real appreciation for his intuitive connection with God. I wondered, *Where did all this come from?* I had not known Andy well during his teen years, and I wasn't aware of his growing grasp on how to do life.

During a group session toward the end of the retreat, we talked about the value of spending regular, personal time alone with God. Everyone agreed that, in theory, time apart with God is a great idea. But most in the group admitted to a rather hit-and-miss experience with it as a personal habit. When Andy's turn came to share, however, his eyes shone as he launched into a description of the regular, personal times he enjoys with God.

Andy described frequent sessions of what he calls focused worship. While reflecting on a passage of Scripture, he selects a particular aspect of God's character highlighted in the passage. Then he meditates on this quality, sings songs to God in honor of it, sits before God in silent worship, and asks God to build that character trait into his life.

As Andy described his times apart with God, I thought, *OK, right. That's it. What I've been sensing in Andy these last couple of days is what others once sensed in Jesus' disciples.* The New Testament book of Acts, speaking of Peter and John, records that the Pharisees "were astonished and they took note that these men had been with Jesus" (Acts 4:13). There is a noticeable quality, an aroma, a set of identifying characteristics that people display who spend regular time in the company of Jesus Christ.

FINGER THE JADE

All of this reminds me of the story of a young boy in China many years ago who wanted to become a master workman in jade. The boy nervously approached the local jade master, and with a deep bow stammered, "Sir, it is my wish to become your apprentice." The master studied the boy for a moment and then instructed him to come back the next day.

The elated boy could barely sleep that night. In the morning, he arrived early but was a little deflated when the master simply instructed him to sit through the day fingering a small piece of jade. This was repeated the next day. And the next. And the day after that. After some weeks, the frustrated young boy gathered his courage and asked his teacher, "Please, Master, when will my lessons begin?" The master nodded and replied, "Tomorrow rewards patience."

The boy returned the following morning, certain that now his real training would begin. His heart sank, however, as his master once again placed an object in his hand. But on this day, instead of jade, the master placed an ordinary stone in the hand of the young boy. Instantly the boy dropped the stone and cried, "But, Master, this is not jade!" "How is it," replied the master, "that you know?"

Without a single word from his teacher, the boy, through direct daily contact with the jade, had begun to become an authority.

This, I think, is what my friend Andy has been experiencing. Little by little, through direct daily contact, apart from the instruction of any teacher, Andy is becoming an authority on Jesus Christ.

"I am the way and the truth and the life. No one comes to the Father except through me" (John 14:6). By spending time with the one the Bible calls "the way," Andy's heart is finding a new and sure direction. By sitting patiently under "the truth," his own life is increasingly ringing true. And by pausing regularly to rest in the presence of "the life," Andy's words and actions are becoming more and more alive themselves. "That which . . . our hands have touched," says the Bible, "this we proclaim" (1 John 1:1). We intimately know best those things we have handled personally.

In whatever place the master has assigned us, our chief business in life is to finger the jade. Seeing, hearing, and touching Jesus is to be woven throughout all the ordinary activities we engage in from day to day. And as Andy discovered, putting aside regular bits of time to sit with him in Scripture reflection and prayer is an important entry point for God into the rest of life. The unhurried listening, attentiveness, and absorption of his Spirit that happen in private times with God tend to introduce his presence into our other involvements too. Personal times apart with God create a sort of enlightened and courageous camaraderie that wafts its aroma out across our whole world.

Spending time one-on-one with God, however, does not always come easily. In their compelling book *The Sacred Romance*, Brent Curtis and John Eldredge touch on the challenge of retreating with God: "As we . . . enter into solitude and silence in our own desert place, the first thing we encounter is not rest, but fear, and a compulsion to return to activity."[1]

This compulsion tends to divert us from our inner lives and push us to the busy surface of things. Thomas Merton had this exterior hubbub in mind when he wrote, "Incapable of the divine activity which alone can satisfy his soul, fallen man flings himself upon exterior things, not so much for their own sake as for the sake of the agitation which keeps his spirit pleasantly numb."[2]

Spending time alone with God is unfamiliar territory for many of us. It's a little like finding ourselves in a foreign country, beset by pressing needs but not knowing how to speak the language. It can be awkward, frustrating, sometimes tense. It can make one-on-ones with God an experience that, without much persuasion, we can usually find ways to avoid.

I distinctly recall some puzzling realizations about myself along these lines in the early days of my relationship with God. I remember the day it occurred to me that, although I loved to talk about God, I didn't much care to talk *with* him. I also realized that, although I liked to read books about biblical subjects, I had relatively little interest in the Bible itself.

I noticed further that if responding to God seemed to be to my advantage, I was eager to do it. But when honoring his promptings became inconvenient or embarrassing or in any way cut against my agenda, I found reasons not to hear his call.

It occurred to me that these inconsistencies were a little strange, but for a while I didn't pay much attention to them. It turned out that these simmering inner contradictions were my first whiff of a classic conflict experienced by all Christians, a spiritual struggle that has come to be known as the Already, Not Yet dilemma.

ALREADY, NOT YET

As Christians, we are *already* children of God, *already* made spiritually alive, *already* drawn to God and desirous of him. Still, in our day-to-day experience, we are *not yet* entirely renewed. We are *not yet* entirely interested in God, trustful of him, or convinced that he is quite what we need. Thus the deep inner tug-of-war hinted at in the last chapter, a war waged for the affections of our restless hearts. The apostle Paul tasted this conflict and wrote, "I do not understand what I do. For what I want to do I do not do, but what I hate I do" (Romans 7:15).

One part of our being is attracted to God. We are engaged and nurtured by him; we feel fulfilled when in his company. But there is another part within that flees God. God feels threatening to us, intimidating. His presence sets off an allergic reaction inside us. We cough and sneeze and convulse and want to get him out of our system.

Nowhere is this inner struggle more evident than when it

comes to spending time alone with God. Our Already reality wants to draw close to God, while the Not Yet part of us wants to run for its life. Maybe our Not Yet part understands that its fate is to gradually diminish as we spend time interacting with God.

Adding to this vexing internal conflict, both the secular and religious cultures around us tend to reinforce the Not Yet part of our experience by feeding it endless foods at odds with intimacy with God.

For example, on the secular side, do you know the three most commonly used words in the English language today? Answer: *Where's the remote?* In such an instant culture, with its emphasis on immediate gratification, it is perhaps not hard to understand why retreating with God, who refuses to operate according to such urgent, self-centered timetables, is not our favorite activity.

Then there is the issue of the competition. A myriad of entertainment, education, self-improvement, and career choices shout for our attention every day. These insistent voices regularly drown out the more patient, quiet voice of God in his bid for our hearts. Many of these choices are good in themselves, but living in America is like swimming in a sea of chocolate. It's great stuff—but it can drown you.

Along with this secular baggage, many of us carry around a fair amount of spiritual baggage that also cuts against intimacy with God. For instance, some of us connect our privilege to draw close to God with our performance for him. The other day I was talking with a friend who lately has been spending an hour every morning in prayer. She was downcast; she was sure God wanted her to spend two. I thought, *Ouch! I have an idea who's driving this performance—and it isn't God.*

The scenario is painfully typical. If we've been accomplishing much for God lately, we have confidence to draw near to him. If we haven't been performing up to our standards (and who can do that?), we feel vaguely guilty and prefer to avoid him.

Other religious bandits also hijack communion with God: there's the notion that only a select few can really expect to experience God intimately—only spiritual leaders or others specially favored by God. Or there's the feeling that everyone else can know God deeply, but not me—I'm different. I'm hopelessly undisciplined, completely unspiritual.

Then there are challenges having to do with the way we are wired. Some people simply have a much harder time with aloneness and quiet than others. Their personalities are built for action and energetic activity. An extended period of quiet (anything beyond about thirty seconds) gives these folks a case of the heebie-jeebies. While on the outside they struggle to enforce a suitably spiritual appearance, on the inside they feel like somebody just let loose a roomful of monkeys.

We could go on to look at lots of other obstacles that muscle us away from God. But maybe it's enough to agree that in a world like ours, with frailties like ours, there will always be a thousand obstacles to spending meaningful time alone with God—the very time our hearts need to become gripped by a vision of the new country to which we are traveling.

The world tends naturally away from God, and we drift with it. Those who want God, and want more than a cool acquaintance with him, will feel themselves swimming against the tide.

Yet we all crave to finger the jade. We're all hungry for personal contact and comfort. Our hearts desire romance and re-creation in God; our spirits want to worship and lounge in his company. "As the deer pants for streams of water, so my soul pants for you, O God. My soul thirsts for God, for the living God. When can I go and meet with God?" (Psalm 42:1, 2).

THE MENU OF THE HEART

In the previous chapter, we noted that our deep inner hungers have the power to push us in unfruitful directions. We also noted, however, that if we ask, God will inject our hunger with a craving for genuine, spiritual food. It is in regularly dining on this menu of the heart, a menu explored in the coming chapters, that we intimately touch and handle, hear and see Jesus Christ for ourselves.

It is told that long ago in a small village in rural England, a man came to town once a week with his two dogs. The Dogman, as the townspeople called him, had taught his two animals, both vicious and strong, to fight savage contests with one another. Each week the Dogman took bets against the townspeople regarding which dog would master the other. One week he backed one dog, and the next week the other. But on whichever animal he placed his wager, the Dogman always won. Finally, the frustrated citizens took him before the local magistrate and accused him of using magic arts to divine the winner, a crime for which, if convicted, the Dogman could lose his life. Forced to give up his secret, the Dogman shrugged and said to the judge: "My lord, there's no magic about it. It is a simple matter. The dog I feed is the dog that wins."

A crude illustration, but apt to our subject. The part of us we feed is the part that wins. Our Already, Not Yet competitors each have big appetites; our challenge is to remind ourselves which one to feed. The hungry heart that sits like a beggar at Jesus' feet will be treated to a banquet for the soul. Such a heart gains strength to overcome the army of obstacles that the world daily marches out against it.

So why should we hesitate? Why not ask God to swell our hunger for the heavenly food? Why not feed our famished hearts on the bread and wine of Heaven—Jesus Christ, the soul's eternal banquet?

Central to this menu of the heart is the unique nourishment of Scripture and prayer. A vibrant experience of God in ordinary life springs from the awareness and courage that take hold of us when our days become seasoned with Scripture and prayer. Without them, this world is just not designed to deliver the insight, power, and direction needed to live in the Already dimension of life.

What then is the path to a rich experience of the Bible and prayer? That is the special focus of the next two sections of this book.

Lord, the challenges of spending time alone with you sometimes push me toward other choices, yet I want that bread and wine that are only found in you. Would you develop a deeper longing in me for you? Would you increase my appetite for spending time at your side? Help me slow down and hear, see, and touch you, the master's rock, my eternal jewel, given to redeem me from all that is Not Yet into all that is Already mine in you.

Amen.

SAVORING HIS WORDS

How sweet are your words to my taste, sweeter than honey to my mouth!

Psalm 119:103

4 LIBERTY

Winter or summer, rain or shine, Bill could be found in the same place, on the corner of First and Main. Propped against the brown brick exterior of Larson's Clothing, under the peeling OshKosh B'Gosh sign, big Bill watched the world go by as he quietly passed his days. As kids we called him "Bill the Bum." Not exactly correct by today's standards, but typical stuff in the mid-1960s in a small town in rural Minnesota. Bill—I never learned his last name—wore heavy farmer coveralls, a winter coat, gloves, and an earflap cap no matter the weather.

"Hey, Bill! How ya doin'?" my friends and I hollered as we biked by. As though slowly returning from a faraway world, Bill lifted his head slightly and languidly raised a gloved hand. Then he retreated into the oblivion from which he had been roused.

In summer Bill slept in the city park or the doorways of shuttered businesses along Main Street. Where he lay down when the snow flew, I don't know.

Forty years later, the image of Bill is still fresh in my mind—quietly shuffling here and there, trying to stay out of the way, muttering nervously, always a bit out of touch. Sometimes Bill was the recipient of small bits of charity, at other times the object of insults or self-righteous clucking. Occasionally he was on the receiving end of a tame prank.

My family moved from that town when I was in junior high. Years later, on a return visit, I learned that Bill had passed away. When I mentioned this to my dad, he surprised me with a bigger picture of Bill's life—Bill had quite a lot of money. He and a sister had inherited a considerable sum on the death of their parents, enough so that Bill could have lived a much more comfortable life than he did.

What's the story? I wondered. Why did Bill sleep for years on park benches, drenched in the rain or shivering through hard Minnesota winters? Why, during summer, did he hang out on the street corner under the broiling sun, always dressed as though just about to leave for the North Pole? Why did Bill eat leftovers and handouts when he could have bought anything he wanted at the town cafe? What was Bill fleeing from? What was he protecting himself from or trying to avoid? What inner demons spoke so convincingly that Bill believed falsehoods sounded like the truth?

I don't know the answers to these questions. I never will. But, somehow, asking them opened a window of awareness into the workings of my own heart. As I pondered Bill's self-imposed poverty, it became plain to me: I am a whole lot like Bill. In God I have everything I need for an abundant life. In him is someone who loves me and has the power to take care of me. In him I have a meaningful future—one designed to stir and express my deepest desires. In God my financial and health needs have an advocate; my relational and emotional longings are fed. In God I am wanted, safe, and loved.

All of this is true, and I enjoy the fruit of it every day. Yet often, like Bill, I find myself shuffling through life, muttering at and obeying my private demons. I ignore my riches in God and feed on stale food. I sleep in the rain and bake in the sun and put on a thousand inappropriate garments to protect myself. With the truth all around me, I live much of my life in retreat from phantom lies.

TOWARD LIBERATION

The Bible understands this human dilemma. It says that Satan is "a liar and the father of lies" (John 8:44) and that the whole world is under his influence (1 John 5:19). It appears it is Satan's business to urge lies upon us that push us to irrational choices and impoverished lives—lives that anxiously struggle against many imaginary dangers and fears. And against these fears, we employ a thousand odd habits and coping devices that make Bill's behavior seem not much more peculiar by comparison.

Some of us have looked for a silver bullet to deliver us from these struggles—the big insight, the major revelation, the defining inner victory. From my perspective, though, I'm not sure there comes any single moment this side of Heaven when we can expect to be entirely set free from our phantoms. As Christians, our inner transformation is an escape of inches, a gradual shedding of old garments and a putting on of our new attire in Christ.

Into our battle for escape, however, God has inserted a key weapon—the Bible. It is the Bible's special ability to slice through the veneer of falsehood that wraps around every subject, revealing the truth that resides inside. In particular, the Bible is powerful in its ability to liberate human souls from the fictions that enslave us. "For the word of God is living and active. Sharper than any double-edged sword, it penetrates even to dividing soul and spirit, joints and marrow; it judges the thoughts and attitudes of the heart" (Hebrews 4:12).

For those who want to increasingly "live into" the truth, the Bible is a gift. The Bible is not a book of morality but a revelation of reality. The Bible is not concerned about dictating a system of dos and don'ts. Instead, it is about revealing the workings of the world in which we live. The Bible's chief gift to humans is the way it reveals that somebody loves us and has the power to escort us to a better country. Someone understands the predicament of being human and has a solution to the dilemma. The Bible tells us clearly who this someone is and how we can increasingly live by his liberating, empowering Spirit.

But what about this Bible? While most Christians hold the Bible in high regard—we often avoid it. Although we believe it holds the promise of our freedom, we spend remarkably little time searching it. The Bible seems intimidating—thick and heavy, filled with unusual language, sometimes hard to understand. Where do we start? How do we interact with it in a way that allows it to do its work of liberation in us?

TASTING AND DIGESTING

There are a wide variety of approaches one can take when dealing with Scripture. They range, on the one hand, from a patient study of original Greek and Hebrew words to something that can approach speed-reading on the other.

Somewhere between these methods is another way. It is an ancient approach that focuses on Scripture as food for one's soul—as bread and wine for hearts hungry for a transforming experience of God. This chapter and the two that follow will introduce you to this simple and life-changing way of reading your Bible. Tasting, slowly chewing, and digesting Scripture in the way we will describe has deep roots in the history of the Christian faith.

Let's allow Jeanne Guyon, a Christian teacher of the sixteenth century, to introduce us to the broad principles of a method of Bible reading she called "praying the Scripture":

> "Praying the Scripture" is a unique way of dealing with the Scripture; it involves both reading and prayer.
>
> Here is how you should begin.
>
> Turn to the Scripture; choose some passage that is simple and fairly practical. Next, come to the Lord. Come quietly and humbly. There, before Him, read a small portion of the passage of Scripture you have opened to.
>
> Be careful as you read. Take in fully, gently and carefully what you are reading. Taste it and digest it as you read.[1]

Taste and digest. I once visited an art museum where I found myself surrounded by gorgeous paintings on every side. The trouble was I didn't see them. A tight schedule had me trotting along so fast that one masterpiece blurred into the next—a deflating way to get some culture! It is this tendency not to see the masterpieces on the pages of Scripture that this method of praying the Scripture tries to address. In reading the Bible like this, we let no artificial schedule push us from one passage to the next. Instead we relax a little, take a breath, and practice noticing the big and small ways God is present and speaking through the passage. If something in the text seems especially meaningful or alive, we stay with it, prayerfully interacting with God, and allowing the rest of the passage to wait until another time.

Guyon continues:

"Praying the Scripture" is not judged by *how much* you read but by the *way* in which you read.

If you read quickly, it will benefit you little. You will be like a bee that merely skims the surface of a flower. Instead, in the new way of reading with prayer, you must become as the bee who penetrates into the depths of the flower. You plunge deeply within to remove its deepest nectar.

. . . Plunge into the very depths of the words you read until revelation, like a sweet aroma, breaks out upon you.[2]

You can see in Guyon's words that in this method of reading the Bible, our concern moves beyond a simple mental scanning of the information toward a deep digesting of the passage. The key, as Guyon describes, is to bite off a small piece of Scripture and chew and chew until it begins to yield nourishment. In this process the "food value" of the passage strengthens and delights the heart, often inspiring us to pause during reading for spontaneous moments of worship, intercession, thanksgiving, or petition—thus the term "praying the Scripture."

When some form is given to this approach, we arrive at a Bible meditation method that follows this general path:

• *Read* the passage several times to get the big picture. What is the main message of the text?

• *Reflect.* What single word, phrase, or impression especially whispers to you from the passage? Ponder whether this is perhaps God's personal word to you at this time. Give this word time to gradually open itself to your mind and heart.

Try this: If the passage describes an event recorded in the Gospels, Acts, or one of the Old Testament historical books, imagine yourself in that scene. Imagine the sounds, smells, weather, time of day, and surrounding activity of the passage. Consider the people involved. What do you see? Get connected with their desires, concerns, attitudes, fears, and needs. If the passage is poetic in nature (a psalm, for example, or portions of many other books), allow the images of the passage to present themselves to your mind and heart.

• *Respond.* Express to God any thoughts, longings, or worship the passage inspires. Respond to God in silent or verbal prayer, journaling, movement (dancing, kneeling, lying prostrate, for example), song, art, or other ways that help you fully express your heart to God.

• *React.* Ask God to help you weave the truth of this passage into your daily life. Ask yourself, "What is one way I will practice God's message to me through this passage this week?"

"Praying the Scripture" in this way holds immense spiritual value. While it is just one among many fruitful ways to read or study the Bible, for hearts starved for intimacy with their Lord it is a path toward rich communion. In the next two chapters, we will probe further the unique soul food that is the Bible.

Jesus, you woke me with a word spoken into my slumbering soul. "Arise," you said. "Walk, see, be healed." The intention of your heart, spoken into me as your word, is the one thing each day that makes me increasingly alive. Open my ears to that word, dear Lord; increase its sweetness to me. Create inside me a growing space where that word is welcome, at home, and in command.

Amen.

5 ENCOUNTER

I was in high school when, one day, a traveling evangelist visited our school. He was great—funny, challenging, and amazingly hip. He invited us to come hear more at a local church the following night, and I decided to go. The evening took an unexpected turn, however, when just minutes into the event it became clear that we had been invited to an old-fashioned record-burning party!

Ouch!

I'd heard about events like these but, as a wannabe musician, had managed to steer clear of them until now. As I gazed at the growing stack of vinyl waiting to be torched, I wondered if there was any way I could possibly save my old friends The Beatles from such an undignified end. As I pondered the problem, I noticed someone across the sea of records, a beautiful blonde-haired girl I'd never seen before. Before the night was over, I had arranged an introduction through a mutual friend and found out her name and the fact that she lived in town. My concern over the fate of John, Paul, George, and Ringo distinctly diminished as I began to puzzle over a new problem— whether I had a chance with The Beautiful Girl.

I faced several challenges. First, The Beautiful Girl seemed a year or two older than me—a huge social difference at seventeen. Her attractive looks represented another problem (since I'm more of the Barney Fife variety). And finally, she was accompanied by a watchful older sister. But something in The Beautiful Girl's manner toward me gave me hope.

At home that night, I looked through the phone book and found a half-dozen households in town with her last name. The next day I set out to see if I could find where she lived. I thought if I just happened to be out for a walk and just happened to see her in the yard, well, who knew which way the wind might blow?

I went here and I went there, gathering little pieces of information as I went. I discovered from her uncle where The Beautiful Girl lived. I learned from someone else that she wasn't, in fact, older than me but—importantly—the same age! Another person let me know what time she might be home. Bit by bit, I gathered information until my facts formed a foundation from which I could mount an offensive to start a relationship with The Beautiful Girl—who eventually became my wife!

Dependable information is an important platform on which to build a relationship. My heart beat fast when I first saw my future wife. But without the aid of some helpful information, I would have been stymied in my pursuit of her. I've discovered this same dynamic in connection with God. Without the information about God that the Scriptures supply, human beings often make wrong assumptions about a relationship with him:

Rats! He's in a higher social class.

He's way too perfect.

He'd never associate with me!

And so on. Discovering the truth about God is an important doorway to intimacy with him. Yet, here's a puzzle: have you ever noticed a tendency to weight your relationship with God toward a ceaseless gathering of information *about him* without ever enjoying the intimacy the information is meant to foster?

My wife, Gerri, and I have now been married for more than thirty great years. But what would have happened if, in those early days, I had simply continued to collect more and more information about her—her likes and dislikes, favorite foods, goals in life, favorite banned-record artist—yet never took the risk to move beyond an informational relationship into something more risky and rewarding? Wouldn't that have been strange? Year after year to simply research The Beautiful Girl but never date her? To watch her from across the street, from the cover of the bushes, with my notebook of Beautiful Girl facts?

Spooky. Yet, in some ways, this is the sort of relationship many of us seem satisfied to have with God. Our association with him often consists simply of an impersonal assortment of mental information we have collected over the years.

CONSUMING THE WORD

An informational versus a relational way of connecting with God has a lot to do with how we interact with the Bible. As we discussed in the last chapter, Bible reading can be either an exercise in accumulating information about God or a means of direct encounter *with* him. In the first instance, our focus goes to ideas, principles, arguments, and explanations—in the second, to meeting the author.

In the method of reading the Bible introduced in the last chapter—praying the Scriptures—the Bible becomes a midwife helping to birth new life inside us. It becomes like the mutual friend who introduced me to my wife on that happy night long ago. Across the Bible's bridges of introduction, I approach Jesus Christ, grasp his outstretched hand, and draw alongside him, encouraged by something in his manner that signals that he wants to know me.

So, while the Bible contains wonderful information about God, our goal is not simply to collect it, sort it, categorize it—conquer it. Our goal is to <u>consume</u> the words of the Bible as <u>food for our hungry souls.</u>

Imagine an orchard at harvesttime. Imagine how puzzling it would be if, after working hard to gather in the fruit, the harvest crew simply left it crated on the ground to rot and moved on to the next orchard, there to do the same. Wouldn't that be strange? Moving from tree to tree, working hard, collecting fruit. Sorting, sizing, boxing, and stacking but leaving it all behind at the end of the day. Yet that is what we do with the Scriptures when we mentally harvest information from a passage yet move on before giving our spirits time to taste, chew, swallow, and digest its fruit.

Let's take this fruity analogy a step further. Imagine a passage of Scripture as though it were an apple. There is <u>no nourishment gained by merely thinking</u> about <u>an apple</u>, peering at it, even studying it. Apples are <u>for eating.</u> Sometimes they are <u>messy.</u> Sometimes, depending on their size or shape, you may <u>not know exactly how to take the first bit</u>e. Sometimes they taste tart and make your lips pucker, and you wonder whether you like the apple you are eating. But eating your apple is the only way to personal nourishment. Food is not for looking at or thinking about, but for eating.

Those of us rooted in the Protestant tradition have, in many ways, inherited a mental approach to faith. Someone once quipped, "They don't call us Protestants for nothing!" We cry at one another from our separate perches: "I protest what you believe!" "Yeah, well, I protest what you just said!" "Oh yeah? Well, I protest your doctrine on that!" "And I protest how you think about that!" And so on and so forth. Sadly, Protestantism's best energy often seems focused on competing with one another to come up with better ways to think about faith.

Beyond Logic

In a way, this should not be surprising. Protestantism sprang up in response to a variety of serious biblical lapses in the church. It was the duty of the early Protestant thinkers to reshape certain abused doctrines, replacing them with ways of understanding faith that were more in line with the scriptural witness. This was a good thing, an important recharting of the ship's direction. But this early focus on a mental, intellectual approach to faith has unfortunately become, in many ways, the Protestant trademark.

There is an old Middle Eastern story of a mystic who went on a journey, taking with him a scholar as his companion. Soon they came to the shore of an ocean. On the other side, God himself stood beckoning. The mystic straightway flung himself into the waves, but the scholar stood on the shore, lost in his reasoning.

The mystic called out to the scholar, "Why do you not follow?"

The scholar answered, "O, brother, my thoughts are in conflict. I dare not advance. I must go back."

The mystic cried again, "Forget what you have read in books. God beckons. Plunge into the water!"

The shelves of Christian bookstores groan under the weight of a never-ending torrent of books designed to continually upgrade our thinking about God. There seems to be an unquestioned assumption among us that if we could just understand God better we would know him better. If we could only clear up our thinking on this, broaden our understanding of that, or perhaps purify our doctrinal position on some other thing, then we would discover the silver bullet of the Christian faith.

But the story of the mystic points us to another way of faith, a way that reaches back before the Protestant Reformation, through the Middle Ages, through the early church, to Jesus himself. It is a less purely mental and more spiritually experiential approach to faith. Consider this difficult statement by Jesus: "I tell you the truth, unless you eat the flesh of the Son of Man and drink his blood, you have no life in you. . . . Whoever eats my flesh and drinks my blood remains in me, and I in him" (John 6:53, 56).

This is the kind of truth one can swim in but not build rational bridges across. It is not a purely logical statement. Oops! Does it appear that I just criticized Jesus' teaching? If it does, might that be because we demand truth to always be rationally comprehensible before diving in? Statements like the one above, however (and many others by Jesus), stretch our minds beyond the bounds of simple logic.

It is not hard to sympathize with Jesus' disciples, who were sometimes reduced to head-scratching. "[The disciples] kept asking, 'What does he mean . . . ? We don't understand what he is saying'" (John 16:18).

Certain Christian truths fall outside the realm of purely rational thinking. They are not irrational but *extra*rational—beyond rational, greater than rational. They communicate realities that must be experienced in order to be understood, truths that must be lived to be comprehended. Concerning such realities any explanation—even explanations by those who have experienced them—always fall a little flat. So if our faith feels a little flat, perhaps it is because we are weighted toward a primarily intellectual, rational, explanatory approach to God.

For those who want to engage Jesus Christ at a deep level, certain words that have fallen into disuse among us must be reintroduced into our spiritual vocabulary, words like *mystery, intuition, communion, meditation, reflection.* These words represent doorways into experiencing God in a way that may be tasted, but not totally described.

"Praying the Scripture," introduced in the last chapter, is an important way to read the Bible because it ushers us toward such a compelling, personal experience of God. Praying the Scripture respects the fact that as humans we are not only thinking beings, we are also—and perhaps more fundamentally—spiritual ones. It understands that as we quietly meditate upon Scripture, our spirits may be feeding long before and after our minds are aware that we are eating. The patience of praying the Bible allows our spirits the leisure needed to interact with the Holy Spirit who meets and ministers to us through the written Word.

Jesus said, "I have much more to say to you, more than you can now bear. But when he, the Spirit of truth, comes, he will guide you into all truth. . . . He will bring glory to me by taking from what is mine and making it known to you" (John 16:12-14). Patient, loving, reflective browsing of the Bible allows the Holy Spirit to make Christ known to our deepest parts. A meditative approach to Scripture respects the fact that, at times, the mind must wait the table while the heart dines.

RESTING IN READING

The four phases of praying the Scriptures outlined in the last chapter—Read, Reflect, Respond, and React—are marked by a listening, prayerful, and responsive way of interacting with the Bible. In this chapter I want to encourage you to experiment with a further way of Bible reading. You can do this by exchanging the final phase, React, for a new one—Rest.

While it is important to respond and react in practical ways to the passages we read, it is equally important to notice those many times during Bible reading when our hearts urge us to temporarily put activity aside and just rest lovingly in God's presence. In the restful, worshiping moments of Bible reading, active thoughts and verbal prayer ultimately give way to simply sitting with God in quiet, loving, wordless communion. Being with God in this way is something like two lovers sitting on the porch swing at the end of the day in silent, loving union, watching the sun go down. It is an intimacy where words become unnecessary—a mutual love that goes beyond expression, a trust in the other that needs no outward assurances.

You may notice yourself feeling drawn to scattered quiet moments like these throughout your Bible reading time, or to a more extended period toward the end. Either way, out of such restful union emerges deep strength and courage for our journey with God.

Recalling the basic stages for Bible reading outlined in the last chapter, a form that includes an emphasis on restful union is as follows:

• *Read* the passage several times to get the big picture. What is the main message of the text?

• *Reflect.* What single word, phrase, or impression especially whispers to you from the passage? Linger over it as perhaps God's special word to you from the text. Let this single word or idea gradually open itself up to you.

See the passage: If you are reading a narrative passage (a story passage), use God's gift of imagination to form a mental picture of the scene. Perhaps imagine looking at the scene through a video camera—zoom in on the various characters or pan across the activity. Imagine the sounds, smells, weather, and time of day. Who is there? Why? What do they want, need, long for, or fear? How are their hopes and desires like yours? If the passage is poetic in nature (the psalms, for example, or portions of many other books) allow the images of the passage to present themselves to your mind and emotions.

• *Respond.* Express to God any thoughts, longings, or worship the passage inspires. Respond to God in ways that help you fully express your heart to God, including verbal prayer, journaling, movement, song, art, or other expressions.

• *Rest.* From time to time, or near the end, put words and activities aside and simply relax before God in loving, wordless, restful communion. Such union with God does not require that we "feel" God. It requires only a loving, open, trustful receptivity to his presence. Such receptivity is roused by the reflective Bible meditation described above and often only requires our permission to express itself.

In the end, the mind wants answers but the heart craves rest. Both needs must be attended to in our gradual transformation in Christ. To our times of mental, analytical study of God, we'll be wise if we add the balancing influence of prayerful, attentive, restful moments when communing with God through Scripture.

Dear Jesus, you are your Father's Word. I want to make a home for your word in me because when I do, I make a home for you. Come abide in me, Lord. Speak meaning, calling, challenge, and hope. Speak the death of old things and the possibility of new. Speak my name, Lord, the name that only you know, the name at the sound of which my heart leaps like a child in the womb in eagerness to be born. This is the power of your word in me.

Amen.

6 UNSTUCK

I have often heard quietly rumored an unusual phenomenon connected to Bibles. Many confidentially share that when they pick up the Bible to read or study, they suddenly experience an odd new fascination with everything else around them.

The magazine that lay unopened on the coffee table since it was put there a week ago suddenly cries to be read. The pattern on the living room carpet that strangely had been overlooked before reveals itself now as clever and worth a long examination. The birds chirping outside the window that only a minute earlier were completely unheard now demand your full attention. What is the mystery of this book, the Bible, that it makes common objects suddenly so interesting, entertaining, and diverting?

Yes, Bible reading generates all sorts of unexpected reactions. Peculiar bouts of sleepiness, daydreams, pressing reminders of errands that need attention, a sense of having fallen inside a vast, spiritual fog. The Scriptures, taken in hand by any ordinary reader, have these effects and many others. Puzzling. Embarrassing. Galling!

Bible reading is loaded with challenges on every side. From language that is foreign to our background and culture, to the constant threat of stumbling upon something new to obey, to a certain underworld personality eager to sabotage our experience, Bible reading can be a tug-of-war. This chapter identifies a variety of obstacles to Bible reading that many people face. With each obstacle are some suggested tips that can help get you unstuck. Hopefully the pointers will address issues relevant to you. (If, by the way, a Bible-reading difficulty you face is not represented in this chapter, let me know. I would love to hear from you!)

Let's spend some time now pondering challenges that confront the typical Bible reader, along with possible solutions.

TIME

Life can be incredibly busy. How do you carve out time to read the Bible?

A discipline imposed from the outside that does not correspond with a desire on the inside soon becomes a constricting, weighty thing. So first, ask God to give you a growing internal hunger for the Bible and time alone with him.

Philippians 2:13 tells us that "it is God who works in you to will and to act according to his good purpose." Ask God to act on your behalf by planting a growing hunger for Scripture in you. Then respond to this hunger by arranging time in your schedule for quiet time with him.

Try this: Create a simple chart dividing each day of the week into twenty-four one-hour periods. For one week, keep careful account of how each hour or perhaps each half-hour is used. Enter your findings on your chart. You may be surprised at how many discretionary hours exist for regular times of oasis with God.

Have you wondered how often to meditate on Scripture, and for how long? If possible, it is very helpful to spiritual growth to spend time every day interacting with Scripture. Three to four times a week would probably be a minimum for those who want to experience increasing intimacy with God.

Many people find that fifteen to twenty-five minutes with a passage of Scripture is enough time to "relax into" the text, allowing stray thoughts and distractions to recede and the Holy Spirit to make the passage alive.

Any amount of time, though, is helpful—even five to seven minutes. When meditating for short periods, consider returning to the same passage several days in a row. The time between the meditations becomes, in a certain sense, part of the meditation. God often enlivens the passage to us in unusual ways during the in-between times. Then we can bring that heightened awareness back with us as we interact with the passage again.

FOCUS

During Bible reading, is your mind often distracted by concerns and stray thoughts? How can you stay focused?

Recently I did an experiment. I allowed my mind to go on autopilot for five minutes. During this period, I counted every stray thought or image that wandered through. In five minutes, I counted approximately eighty-five different thoughts or impressions! That's just an interesting piece of trivia until you take into consideration that this is the same mind I must discipline to meditate on Scripture. Whew!

So what do we do? How do we corral our minds for concentrated periods of attention given to Bible reading?

Well, to begin, it is probably not possible to live in a mentally distracted, wandering manner twenty-three hours a day and then immediately hope to become focused and attentive when we pick up our Bibles. Focus begins in the times *between* Bible readings. Try to avoid the constant need for distracting entertainment or other diversions to babysit your mind. Instead, practice bringing the restless concerns that are usually the source of wandering thoughts under the umbrella of God's truth and care throughout your whole day (see 2 Corinthians 10:5). As you do, you will notice a gradual inclination of your mind to focus with delighted attention on the things of God.

A practical aid to staying focused in Bible reading is to write down your reactions to the whisperings of the Holy Spirit as you meditate. Journaling makes your thinking concrete, harnessing thoughts that would otherwise drift away. People who journal are amazed at the frequency and depth with which they seem to be able to hear God's voice.

A wonderful side benefit to journaling is the written witness you are compiling of God's faithful and fruitful activity in your life. This witness can be revisited during difficult times, serving as a reminder that God never leaves or forsakes you.

If falling asleep during Bible reading is a problem for you, try these suggestions:

• Get proper rest. This may even mean the early retirement of the remote control the night before!

• Do something physical to ward off "holy hypnosis." Drink a cup of coffee while meditating on Scripture, take a walk, or move around to express the feelings that Scripture stirs within.

• Jump-start your spiritual engine in preparation for Bible reading with devotional books, Christian biographies, worship CDs, songbooks, or reflections on God in nature.

• Notice the time of day that you are most alert, and arrange your Bible meditation as close to that time as possible.

• Write out what God seems to be specially speaking to you through his Word.

DIGGING IN

The Bible is a big book, and sometimes it can seem overwhelming. Where should you start? How do you decide which passages to read or study or meditate on?

Since Jesus Christ demonstrates to us most clearly who God is and how we may know him intimately, many believe that the Gospels (which are chiefly about Jesus) should be the central focus of Bible meditation. Personally, I tend to divide my Bible reading into the following very approximate percentages: 40 percent Gospels, 30 percent the remainder of the New Testament, and 30 percent the Old Testament. It's hard to choose! It is all grade-A material! There are no hard rules. But something close to these percentages will give you a healthy diet of Scripture.

DEAD OR ALIVE?

What if your Bible reading seems cold and stale, and the passages irrelevant to everyday life? How can you keep your times with Scripture fresh and alive?

There is no more important habit, in regard to making the

Bible come alive, than to practice the truths you encounter in Scripture. Until you begin to *do* the Bible in daily life, reading it usually remains a rather academic chore.

If you had a hobby that you only read about and never practiced, that hobby would soon become abstract and boring. On the other hand, if you practiced your hobby, it would come alive to you, and you would be eager to read any new material that could help you master it more fully.

The same is true of faith. If you practice the truths you read about in the Bible, your faith takes on a sense of adventure that makes further Bible reading extremely desirable. The more we risk living the Bible's message, the more enthralling that message becomes.

And don't forget, before reading Scripture, to pause and invite God to sharpen your mind, soften your heart, and open pathways between the passage you are about to read and your own life situation.

One last tip to help you keep your Scripture reading fresh: for mental stimulation, intersperse different Bible-study methods into your devotions from time to time. A few of these include the study of key people, topics, or words of the Bible; the character qualities of God; the miracles or parables of the Bible; the verse-by-verse, paragraph-by-paragraph, or chapter-by-chapter study of key books; and published Bible studies.

WHO'S TALKING?

Have you wondered how to discern God's voice when you are reading the Bible? How do you know which passages apply to you and which do not?

This, of course, is a question that could take up an entire chapter—or an entire book. But a couple of rules of thumb might be helpful.

First, all Scripture, properly interpreted, forms a framework for life. So there is a sense in which every passage of the Bible applies to me. The issue becomes one of timing and application.

For example, a book describing the principles of basketball contains instructions applicable to everyone who wants to learn to play basketball. Yet there is a proper sequence and progression concerning which drills to practice when. The reader is really in need of a good coach to help personalize and apply the lessons.

It is the same with Scripture. All the lessons are applicable, but you need to fix your ears on your coach for timing and application. "But when he, the Spirit of truth, comes, he will guide you into all truth. He will not speak on his own; he will speak only what he hears, and he will tell you what is yet to come. He will bring glory to me by taking from what is mine and making it known to you" (John 16:13, 14).

Most of us would love to discover some kind of formula for understanding which Scriptures apply in what ways to our lives. What God is more interested in, it seems, is for us to be attentively connected to him as our personal coach and tutor. This underscores the fact that faith is not primarily about developing a better understanding of truth or more perfectly biblical behavior, but about vibrant, ongoing personal interaction with God.

A TASTE FOR HIS WAYS

Someone once told me he sometimes avoids reading the Bible because he's afraid what it might tell him to do! How can you get over a fear or distaste for God's commands?

Moses might have something helpful to teach us in this regard. Moses began his career with God by nearly getting himself killed, so badly did he want to escape God's will for him (Exodus 3, 4). By the time his ministry ended, however, the Bible says of Moses, "No prophet has risen in Israel like Moses, whom the LORD knew face to face. . . . No one has ever shown the mighty power or performed the awesome deeds that Moses did in the sight of all Israel" (Deuteronomy 34:10, 12).

That's quite a transformation! What happened between the beginning of Moses' career, when he so desperately wanted to avoid God's commands, and the end of it, when he was so fully God's servant?

There does not appear to be any single moment of

transformation in Moses' life. Instead, inch by inch, reluctantly yet regularly, Moses put himself in the place where God was active. As Moses experienced the power of God to transform situations, he developed a taste for God's ways. God proved himself to Moses, and Moses gradually exchanged a fear of God's activity for a heightened desire for it.

If you risk responding to God's overtures through Scripture, you will find yourself, like Moses, wooed into a new way of life—one you will eventually prefer over the limited and self-protective approach that comes naturally to you. God will increasingly whet your appetite for a richer diet of *his* life.

CONNECTING

Finally, what if you find it hard to put yourself into the biblical scene as you read because you are not familiar with the times, dates, and cultural context of the events you're meditating on? What Bible study tools can help you understand these things better?

There are lots of great resources that can help you familiarize yourself with daily life during Bible times. One example is *The New Manners & Customs of Bible Times*,[1] which gives a wonderful overview of life during the biblical era, including domestic life, food, earning a living, geography, climate, travel, social and political groupings, government, warfare, leisure, religion, and more.

Other useful resources include Old Testament and New Testament surveys. These give an in-depth look at the social, political, and religious events surrounding particular books of the Bible. A Bible atlas is a colorful and engaging tool that sheds light on the climate and geography of Bible lands and how these have impacted biblical events. Last are Bible commentaries. The main function of a Bible commentary is to aid in understanding the meaning of Scripture passages, but it also often describes the cultural, political, and geographic forces that shaped biblical events. (A thought: Be careful not to rely too heavily on commentaries to interpret passages for you. You may miss the opportunity to hear something alive and personal from God.)

Unstick me, Lord! How often when I try to read your Word do my mind and heart become gripped by a hundred distracting problems! Jesus, you know my sticking points and the struggle and discouragement I sometimes feel. Come alongside me in my Scripture reading. Speak guidance and power and freedom into our time together. From this day forward, Lord, I believe you will grow an increasing richness, fruitfulnesss, and joy in those precious times I come to meet you in your Word.

Amen.

THE FLAVOR OF INTIMACY

If anyone hears my voice and opens the door,
I will come in and eat with him, and he with me.

Revelation 3:20

7 TRANSPARENCY

The telephone rang at two on a Tuesday afternoon.

"Good afternoon. Is this Mrs. Warne?" asked an emotionless voice at the end of the line.

"Yes."

"Mrs. Warne, this is the Plymouth Police Department."

"Oh?"

"Mrs. Warne, do you know the whereabouts of your son, David, last Saturday night?"

"Last Saturday night?"

"That's right, ma'am. Halloween night."

Oh great! Gerri thought.

The officer explained the reason for his interest. It

appeared that on Halloween night, some junior high kids (so far, David fit the profile) had pelted an apartment building with rocks, one of which struck and broke a window in a second floor stairwell—a seven-hundred-dollar window!

"Well, officer, I'll check with David," Gerri said. "But honestly, that doesn't sound like something he would be mixed up in."

"Yes, ma'am, that's what some of his friends have told us, ma'am. But there are others who say he was involved, ma'am."

Gerri assured the officer we'd speak with David and get back to him.

When our son came home from school, we nonchalantly floated the subject before him. I thought I detected a millisecond of alarm in David's eyes before he coolly assured us he had nothing to do with the incident.

Well, what do you do? Having seen on TV that a coerced confession is no good in a court of law, Gerri and I decided not to press the subject further at that moment. Instead, I simply covered some obligatory ground about honesty being more important than a momentary lapse of judgment. In response, David nodded earnestly and expressed a touching dismay that anybody could act so disrespectfully toward another person's property. And he repeated that he certainly had nothing to do with rocks and windows on Halloween night.

Gerri reported the status of our investigation to Officer Friday, and we went on with life.

A few days later, Gerri was in our minivan on an errand to the store with David and our daughter, Monica. Monica and Gerri were engrossed in conversation in the front seat when suddenly a cry erupted from the rear.

"I did it!"

"Huh?" Gerri responded, peering into the rearview mirror.

"I did it!" cried David. "I broke it!"

Gerri had almost forgotten the incident of a few days before.

"You broke what?"

"The window. The big window."

"What! You mean the apartment window? No!" Gerri found herself saying with disbelief. "You said you didn't do it!"

"I lied! I broke it!" groaned David, breathing hard. "I'm sorry."

Over time, David shared about the days of anxious misery he had spent trying to appear cool on the outside while hiding a secret that continually harassed and accused him within. In the end, the pressure was too much, and David bravely punctured the deception that was suffocating him, slicing it through with the truth. He had to face the music, but at least he could breathe again!

HIDING

Have you ever hidden something important from somebody? Hiding takes a lot of energy. They say of soldiers who must hide from an enemy in war situations that they often experience a nearly overwhelming desire to reveal their location. Apparently, hiding does not sit well with something deep inside us.

Pretending to be something that contradicts our inner reality creates great tension. Pretending breeds a confused and anxious inner experience that dangles us, immobile, between what we know to be true and how we prefer to appear to a watching world.

Christians are in an unusual position regarding the pitfalls of pretending. As people who are continually shedding an old way of life for a new reality in Christ, we are in the constant process of changing who we are. This involves trying to figure out which ideas to embrace and which to reject, what realities to cling to and from which to flee.

For Christians, being authentic is not as simple as merely lining up our outer actions with our inner impulses. You may have noticed that these same inner urges are ones we must often reject, while the new impulses we are called to adopt in Christ sometimes still feel foreign, puzzling, and unnatural. So who are we exactly? When are we pretending and when are we being real? How do we increasingly live toward our new reality in Christ while not denying the truth of our present reality within?

This is no easy question for bankers and carpenters, mechanics and accountants, grocery clerks and computer programmers—regular people who are called upon from moment to moment to discern down which path lies their new, emerging identity in Christ and which path leads back to the familiar realities of an old life passing away.

Sometimes, in a desire to show God (and perhaps other Christians) that we are making progress in our new life in Christ, we unintentionally paper over the remains of the old life we are trying to leave behind. Fears, hurts, disappointments, and pains; confusion, addictions, and sinful obsessions—these messy loose ends represent a way of life we feel we should be free of by now. Consequently, we experience a temptation to hide them from God, others, and even ourselves. But if we do, we separate them from the very one who desires to love us into a new way of being.

One day, a few months before I got my driver's license, I grabbed the keys to my parents' station wagon from the kitchen counter and hopped outside and into the car. I spent the next ten minutes shuttling the car up and down our long driveway (anything to be in control of a moving vehicle, I guess). Well, I got a little cocky at one point and drove forward too quickly, striking the frame of the garage door. The whole house shook. I jerked the car into park and jumped out. Amazingly, there was no discernible damage to the garage or the car.

In a second or two, my mother and older brother rushed from the house to see what had happened. It was obvious that I'd hit the garage. But in a flash I struck on a plan. *Deny it!* So I did. Vehemently. They knew better, of course, but I wouldn't change my story. A barrier was erected between us by my dishonesty that only wore away after a very long time.

Few dynamics have the power to freeze relationships like hiding things from one another. This is especially true in a relationship with God. It's a kinship that cries out for honesty, vulnerability, and transparency—a see-through heart. Intimacy with God does not attempt to hide our messes from God.

God's intense desire to be near us, to share in those things that distress us most, leads him to knock at the door of our unresolved messes—our confusions and weaknesses, our sinful habits and lingering pains. Paradoxically, the way forward into new life in Christ is to invite him into the remains of our old life. There he comforts and kills, consoles and consumes, destroys and re-creates. A see-through heart is one short step away from a re-created heart.

SEE-THROUGH HEARTS

In the Gospels, Jesus shows himself to be a safe person with whom to be transparent—even when it means probing him with frank skepticism:

Philip found Nathanael and told him, "We have found the one Moses wrote about in the Law, and about whom the prophets also wrote—Jesus of Nazareth, the son of Joseph."

"Nazareth! Can anything good come from there?" Nathanael asked.

"Come and see," said Philip.

When Jesus saw Nathanael approaching, he said of him, "Here is a true Israelite, in whom there is nothing false" (John 1:45-47).

The next verses tell us that Jesus observed Nathanael before meeting him and liked what he saw—honest skepticism and all (John 1:48-50).

The Bible is full of stories of those who risked being real with God and received power, comfort, and courage in response. When God called Moses to duty, for example, Moses poured forth his deep fears and objections. These were fielded by God in a compassionate exchange that ultimately gave Moses all he needed to move ahead (Exodus 3, 4).

The psalms are the Bible's Mount Everest of transparency. Many of the psalms were written by King David and show us a man of deep emotion. Typical of David's see-through heart are lines like these from Psalm 6:

Be merciful to me, LORD, for I am faint;

O LORD, heal me, for my bones are in agony.

My soul is in anguish.

How long, O LORD, how long?

. . . .

I am worn out from groaning;

all night long I flood my bed with weeping

and drench my couch with tears.

My eyes grow weak with sorrow;

they fail because of all my foes.

. . . .

The LORD has heard my cry for mercy;

the LORD accepts my prayer.

—vv. 2, 3, 6, 7, 9

Not only pains and sighings but wonderful joys find free expression in the Bible. David dances with abandon before God (2 Samuel 6:12-15), the Shulammite melts at the touch of her lover, a type of Christ (Song of Songs 1:1-4), and our fellow heavenly citizens collapse and cry out, overcome before the glory of God (Revelation 11:15-17). Are we allowed, like these brothers and sisters, to express such delight in God? Of course. Just try to avoid knocking over the furniture as you dance around the room.

Jesus himself revealed a startling transparency that I find inspiring and comforting. Hebrews 5:7 tells us, "During the days of Jesus' life on earth, he offered up prayers and petitions with loud cries and tears to the one who could save him from death, and he was heard because of his reverent submission."

Loud cries and tears. Jesus Christ? *Why?* Because sometimes that is what expressing the real emotions of life calls for. Isn't there help for us in Jesus' example? Doesn't it give us permission to vent our own deep emotional storms to God— the same ones our elder brother was at times moved to express in painful utterances to his Father?

STOPPED-UP SOULS

If God is for transparency and the results of it are so good, why is it often hard to be fully real with God? Your reasons may be different than mine, but I am aware of struggling with transparency on several levels.

First, I am often not aware of a *need* to be transparent. I am often not fully in touch with the many sore spots hidden in my soul that long for God's comfort. Recently, I watched a fascinating documentary about volunteers training for the elite armed forces unit the Navy Seals. Early in training, each volunteer undergoes a torturous experience called Hell Week. Here, trainers push the volunteers to the limits of physical and mental endurance in an attempt to mold them into a cohesive unit. At any time during Hell Week, any volunteer who has had enough can grasp a white towel, always present, signaling that he wants out. One of the trainers in the program said his hardest job all week is to create a constant stream of demands to keep the volunteers distracted and disoriented so they won't have time to reflect on the craziness of the experience and decide to opt out.

I thought, *Wow! What a picture of my life!* How often does Satan disorient me through distracting busyness, keeping me from becoming aware of my inner sore spots and the privilege I have to find comfort in Christ? Sometimes I need to grab the white towel, retreat from tyrannical urgencies, and give attention to the health of my soul.

Another challenge to transparency is the risk and uncertainty involved in inviting God into our pains, sins, and general messes. We wonder, *Where might this lead? What might be required? How do I navigate this unfamiliar territory?* In addition, once stirred, our messes tend to get messier before they get neater. Before, when we pretended they didn't exist, our inner issues may have inflicted just a low-level pain at the edges of our awareness. But now, after acknowledging and beginning to deal with them, they throb so badly we can hardly concentrate on anything else. In the short term, we are tempted to wonder, *Is this worth it?*

Another reason it's hard to be transparent with God is

because so few people model to us that it can and should be done. Most public Christian prayers, for example, give very little insight into how to be real with God. Many are not, in fact, prayers at all, but mini sermons intended to teach, inspire, or impress, presented like three-act plays. In act 1, we meet the characters; in act 2, we are told about the conflict or crisis faced. And in act 3, we learn the expected resolution. Quick and neat (sometimes not so quick), these prayers do not help much in modeling how to unveil our soul's deep places to God.

Years ago I did, in fact, witness a wonderfully transparent prayer. My reaction, however, was telling. I was with a half-dozen people praying for some hurting friends. Suddenly, one of our group began to groan and weep loudly over those for whom we were praying. My response? I immediately leaned over, put my hand on his shoulder, and tried to console him. I was uncomfortable with his anguish and wanted to tidy things up. I was entirely out of touch with the deep spiritual and emotional nature of what was going on. I had yet to learn that some prayers need to rise from the roots of our souls, sometimes carrying awkward expressions of pain and longing with them.

INSIDE OUT

Developing a comfort level with praying outside the box is a key toward experiencing nourishing, healing transparency with God. By "outside the box," I mean praying in ways that you probably have never seen modeled or prayed yourself yet express what is really going on within. Two examples come to mind.

I know a woman who suffered sexual abuse growing up. For many years, this was a taboo subject between her and God. The confused pain and embarrassment she felt, along with hurt questions about how God could let such a tragic thing befall an innocent little girl, made the subject too combustible to speak with God about. For many years she tried to live a happy relationship with God, pretending to be unaware of this elephant in the living room. Her pain often escaped, however, in angry, sideways directions, inflicting its wrath on herself and others—but never God.

There came a time, however, when the woman bravely faced the many questions surrounding these violations. One important day, she allowed herself to share with God the angry bewilderment she had suppressed for nearly thirty years. At one point in her prayer, she imagined herself sitting on God's lap. Then, in her mind's eye, she began to beat on God's chest with angry, clenched fists. In that moment she had crossed a line. Not only had she rebelled against the no-talk rule that had governed this subject for so much of her life, she had also dared express her truest feelings to God. She wondered whether she would be rejected by an angry, offended God. Instead, she was surprised to find another picture forming in her mind—an image of a sorrowing Father who spoke words like "Go ahead, little one. Beat on me. I can take it. I will receive your blows for as long as you need." Having finally trusted her Father with a see-through heart, this woman was embraced with the beginnings of a tender healing that is still expanding today.

Another example is personal, an experience with transparency that I am still digesting. A while ago, for some weeks, I noticed myself hovering at the edge of a strong desire to weep. About what, I didn't know. There was nothing especially sad going on in my life at that time. Besides, I am not much of a crier. So this pull toward tears was mystifying, even a little concerning. I thought, *No, wait—I'm strong. What is this nonsense? Go away, you strange feeling. This isn't how I operate. Besides,* I reminded myself, *mature Christian men don't allow themselves to sink into tears for no particular reason. This smells like self-pity, and what might that lead to? A man could start to cry and never stop!* With thoughts like these, I successfully kept my heart at bay—for a while. But as the philosopher Pascal has said, "The heart has its reasons, which reason does not know."[1] And what my mind at that moment struggled not to know was that God was wooing me to meet him in a time of tears.

In the midst of this unusual struggle, I read about a small, hunchbacked Russian woman, caught up in the Holocaust during World War II. In a holding camp, awaiting the train that would take her to her death, it was her habit to move among the other prisoners, offering spiritual comfort and doing what she could to relieve their suffering. One day the woman spoke of the deep anguish that her calm exterior disguised. As she surveyed her fellow prisoners and hopeless situation, the hunchbacked woman stared searchingly at a friend and said, "I would like, oh, I really would like, to be able to swim away in my tears."[2]

That did it. Somehow the lament of this grieving woman sliced deep into me and opened to full force a torrent of tears in my own heart. Over the next days, I permitted myself to acknowledge a reservoir of pain that I did not realize I had been storing up for a long, long time. And only then did I begin to understand the reasons for my tears.

I cried for many things. For hurting family and friends. For tragedies and crises nearby and far away. For powerless victims everywhere—alone, confused, frightened. I cried for my long-dead Russian hunchbacked sister. I cried for the daily crucifixion of truth—a way of life in the culture in which I live. And I cried for the deep sense of personal fracture I often feel. Because, though I am no longer lost, having been found in Christ, there is still a lostness which courses through my thoughts and behaviors, constantly harassing the budding "foundness" of my relationship with God.

It was not easy to let myself cry, to leak such deep,

unvarnished pain. It did not match assumptions I had about what it meant to be me. But a rejection of those expectations led to an experience with Christ the full implications of which are still working themselves out many months later. God met me in my river of tears.

Or, as it became plain to me over time, I met him in his. He who wept over Jerusalem, who called out to his Father during the days of his earthly ministry with loud cries and tears, has wept an ocean of tears over the world's pain and perplexity—including mine. I wept with the friend of Heaven in an intimate, redemptive grief that helped salve my own pain as I shared with him the weight of his own. A mystery, a privilege, and deeply consoling.

And I was reminded that this is intimacy with God—this letting go, this admitting what I feel and following my heart into the heart of God. How often do I dare go there? In the face of a chorus of objections flung up by my reluctant mind, or the culture—or sadly, even the church—how often do I dare meet Christ in the secret, unnamable place to which he calls me?

"The heart has its reasons, which reason does not know." Our spirits, made alive by the Holy Spirit, constantly urge us into deeper country. The map of this land is only partial and uncertain, but we are sons and daughters of God, led by a Spirit living deep within.

Where is that Spirit calling you presently?

What does your heart yearn for today? What are you hungry or thirsty for? Where, perhaps, do you hurt? What joy do you long to express? In the deep, deep roots of your life, what is stirring? What is important? What could you be sharing with God?

Jesus himself waits at the center of your hunger, your pain, your secret yearning—hoping you'll risk the journey within.

Father, I'm so often afraid that who I am is unworthy to be known. But it hurts to hide. Is it safe to reveal myself to you? Can I let fall away my tense, wearying disguises and simply be with you as your imperfect, loving child? See my heart, Father: it's as foolish as sin, but still it longs for you; it's as heavy as stone, but weary of bearing its burdens alone. Can it be, Father, that this frail heart, the only one I have to offer, is the very one you love?

Amen.

8 LISTENING

Recently a few of us were discussing the question of hearing God. One fellow quipped, "Yes, we all want to hear God speak to us—so we can weigh his opinion against our other options." A droll insight by someone who has been around the block with God.

Humans are eager to hear from God because we correctly sense that in that voice is comfort, affirmation, guidance, and strength to face life. Sometimes, I suppose, we listen with one ear covered in case he should speak something to upset our plans. Yet among those tuned to spiritual things, there is probably no subject that generates more eager interest than the question of how to hear God's voice.

While hearing God is a precious thing, there is something about simply listening that is actually of more interest to me. Beyond hearing specific messages from God, the postures of the heart associated with listening lead, by their very nature, to a deeper rapport with God. Communion, affectionate closeness, attentive intimacy with God—these are the key gifts of listening.

So this chapter is about listening to God—which is to say that it is about reminding my heart to wait, more and more, in loving attention upon him. Let's ponder this subject by offering thoughts in response to the following question: "What are some helps to developing a more attentive ear for God?"

EXCHANGING AGENDAS

Have you ever noticed that the communication habits we use with each other are precisely those that either help or hurt intimacy with God? A particular communication skill of mine, practiced diligently through many years of marriage, was to finish my wife's sentences for her or, failing that, to launch a response before she could complete a remark. The few times Gerri gently pointed this out, I genuinely felt she did not understand that this was simply how some people communicate. I was not doing anything out of the ordinary, I assured her. Certainly nothing rude. This was just how busy people talked.

Some years ago, Gerri and I loaded up the car and eased out of the driveway to begin a road trip to visit relatives in a neighboring state. Our kids were finally at the age when we could leave them home alone without increasing our property insurance, and the idea of a trip with just the two of us was a dreamy tonic to a busy schedule. We looked forward to a leisurely six-hour drive filled with reading, snoozing, and pleasant chitchat.

I waited to get about a block and a half from home before I cut Gerri off in conversation for the first time. This time her response lacked its usual appealing gentleness. She responded sharply, "Joel, I'm tired of you constantly interrupting me before I have finished speaking! It's insulting. It makes me feel you don't respect me or value what I have to say. You are so focused on your own agenda that you don't hear what other people are saying!"

Ouch!

Sometimes the truth rings true. I finally heard Gerri on this subject. But I was bummed. Her reprimand led to a long discussion (happy euphemism) and a noticeably less-carefree car trip. The timing of the truth can be so inconvenient! But her words became central in my conversion toward a more listening ear.

Truly listening to someone requires releasing your own agenda. It requires at least a temporary emotional surrender of your preferred position in favor of a real consideration of the other's interests, needs, or perspectives. This may be what makes listening to God so difficult and sometimes threatening. We are often so married to our own agendas that we mentally construct the message we want to hear from God, ignoring, or perhaps even fleeing, any other. In a sense, we finish God's sentences for him or remind him of our agenda while he is still speaking.

Hearing God requires patient, open-minded, brave listening. It requires releasing safe agendas and stepping through sometimes scary doorways into a bracing new world that fills our lungs with heavenly air. The first result of listening is perhaps not hearing but becoming liberated from small personal programs we have clung to for years as essential to our well-being. These programs are often little tyrants from which we need to be set free if we are to become whole people in Christ.

Being Present to God

I attended seminary some years ago to do academic work to lay a foundation for the spiritual formation work I do today in classes, retreats, and small groups. As I neared completion of that degree, I had conversations, from time to time, with fellow students who planned to continue their work toward further degrees in various directions.

Though I didn't intend to work in their fields, the idea of a further degree tugged at me a bit. The classes looked great, and I liked the sense of challenge. My insecurities were also whispering. An additional degree would make me feel better about myself and buff my sheen a little in the eyes of others. The extra degree would have required, though, at least another twelve to eighteen months of work and thousands of dollars in tuition.

So, what to do? If I really needed the degree, the additional time and money would certainly be well invested. Yet, was it truly necessary? Arguments could be made in both directions.

During those days I took that issue, along with many others, and did something that proved very helpful—I simply made them present to God. I did not particularly ask God what to do; I did not obsess over the subject; I did not seek hard for an answer. I simply brought them regularly into his presence.

The seminary I attended housed a large chapel. In that chapel, I spent many hours slowly walking its perimeter, bringing my life, family, future, and my unresolved questions into the presence of God. Worship, meditation, praise, thanksgiving, and a light sense of holding my "stuff" gently and lovingly in God's presence during those chapel walks gave me an assurance that the Holy Spirit was being given free access to my world. I didn't know exactly where things were headed, but I was confident of his company.

Regarding the specific question of my degree, one day, very offhandedly, I mentioned my growing intention to pursue an additional degree to a local ministry leader I had never met before. She looked at me oddly and asked what the value of all that extra money and work would be to my particular calling. In that moment, somehow the issue became much clearer. I believe God spoke through that woman whom I had never met before and have not seen since. And I believe that my habit of making that subject present to God, accompanying it with an open, impartial, loving, and restful release, made my mind ripe to hear a word from God when it came.

We typically do not invest patient, extended amounts of time listening to God. Feeling terribly pressed by time and events, such listening almost seems like an irresponsible luxury. Yet only through listening does God's will for us begin to appear clear, attractive, and possible. After attentive listening to God, messages from the culture and Satan that previously seemed to require our submission begin to dissolve and lose their power to dictate our lives.

In the instance of my seminary work, for example, I wonder how many hundreds of hours of labor I ultimately became free to invest in my real call by hearing and living God's agenda rather than my own? I have noticed in recent years that through patiently making my life present to God, I have exchanged well over half the activities of my life that once felt necessary (though unfulfilling and unfruitful) for those called and supported by God.

If These Wounds Could Talk

Last week, a woman at my church shared a remarkable story about how God recently spoke to her. She said that his voice was so real she actually looked around the room to see who had spoken.

That is how I like to hear from God. Startling. Direct. Nearly audible. There is a little hitch in my case, however. It doesn't happen. Well, rarely. (You'll notice that I had to tell someone else's story rather than my own.) No, I tend to hear God in less dramatic ways. And one way I have learned to hear him in recent years is in the very areas of my life that I used to think were proofs of his absence—my pain, confusion, and unresolved longings.

As we noted in previous chapters, fallen humans on the road to redemption are home to a wide variety of hungers, thirsts, frustrations, longings, hurts, and confusions. Our typical tendency is to ignore or try to fix these areas. Confusion does not feel holy. Failures do not seem very mature. Unfulfilled desires don't register as spiritually grown up. We generally just want these things to go away (preferably by a dramatic act of God, thereby giving us a victory to broadcast).

But might there be a different approach to these soul wounds? What about acknowledging them? What about becoming comfortable with their presence? And then, how about entering them, resting there, and listening as God's voice speaks out of the heart of them?

Our longings are wise. Our confusions can reveal truth. Our pain and hurts have much to teach. Is it possible, rather than fleeing from or medicating these inner realities, to enter into them, and once there to patiently and lovingly make ourselves present to God's voice through them? A doctor probes our wounds for the truth of our condition. What truths would God speak out of our wounds if we would listen?

SAINTS AND SINNERS

I used to employ a foolproof method to avoid hearing inconvenient words from God sent my way through others. If God's message through others came wrapped in the messenger's anger, impatience, or any other characteristic that rubbed me the wrong way, I would disqualify the core truth within and proceed through life unchecked by God. This "fitness of the messenger" yardstick was a handy criterion, affording me many a light skip past the counsel of God.

In this regard, however, I had the misfortune of being married to an astute woman. There came a day when Gerri exposed my little game to me, and the voices of saints and sinners have since been used by God to communicate truth to me many times.

What is easy about listening to God, through others, for you? What is hard? Depending upon your makeup, you may experience different challenges. When God's word through others feels threatening, our first challenge is to resist the temptation to immediately reject it in an attempt to protect ourselves. On the other hand, those overeager to please others sometimes automatically receive into their deep places too many words as though from God without quietly, patiently discerning the source.

Many, many words are spoken to us each day from a variety of people with varying motivations. Not all contain counsel from God. If we keep our identity and self-image parked securely in him, those words through others that are from God will usually have a confirming feel to them. They will tend to simply underscore, or coalesce into words, certain ideas that have been brewing at the edges of our awareness. On the other hand, words that seem to come out of nowhere should probably be more closely scrutinized as to origin.

Humility permits the receipt of a pregnant word from God through others. Pride attempts to disregard it. Silence gives space for the word to find a home or leave by the way it came.

ACTING TO HEAR

When I was in my early twenties, I pondered joining a ministry being developed under the leadership of a charming, dynamic Christian man. There seemed a lot to like as I looked on from the outside, and I was hot to get involved. Yet somewhere inside me brewed a vague hesitation.

One night, during this time, I had a dream. In it I was treading water in a vast, steely sea. Suddenly at my side was the smiling face of the leader of the ministry I was considering joining. As the man looked at me with a fixed, glassy smile, he proceeded to push my head under the waves. I struggled against him for a while and then woke up.

What an inconvenient dream! Emotionally, I had begun, more and more, to identify my future with this ministry. Was this dream now questioning that? Well, if it was, I decided not to listen. Although the dream seemed to confirm some unseen things I sensed about the quality and safety of this organization, I shrugged it off. I ignored what I now understand was God's confirmation of my apprehensions and signed on to work in the organization. The next few years proved the wisdom of that dream. My refusal to respond was a devaluing of God's guidance that I had much reason later to regret.

My point here is not about the guidance of dreams but about acting on the direction God floats our way. Someone has observed that God remains silent about additional guidance until we have responded to the guidance he has already given. An integral part of listening is responding—acting, doing. Jesus said, "Whoever has my commands and obeys them, he is the one who loves me. He who loves me will be loved by my Father, and I too will love him and show myself to him" (John 14:21).

Jesus reveals himself to those who risk responding to the daily hints and nudges of heaven. For the obedient, an awareness of God's presence and activity becomes greater and greater. George MacDonald, the remarkable Scottish storyteller of the 1800s, was a keen advocate of obedience as the doorway into God's deeper country. "There is no teacher like obedience," said MacDonald, "and no obstruction like its postponement."[1] Later chapters will probe the value of a responsive heart more fully. For now, we will simply note that responding to God's guidance is a good way to keep our ears open.

IMAGINE THAT!

Mark's Gospel account of Jesus' healing of the blind man, Bartimaeus, is compelling on several levels. A particular portion of the text especially sets my mind turning around the question of listening to God: "When [Bartimaeus] heard that it was Jesus of Nazareth, he began to shout, 'Jesus, Son of David, have mercy on me!' Many rebuked him and told him to be quiet, but he shouted all the more, 'Son of David, have mercy on me!'" (Mark 10:47, 48).

The blind man, Bartimaeus, heard that Jesus of Nazareth was nearby. He couldn't see him but, sensing Jesus' presence, he began to cry out for help. In response, a virtual hail of voices pummeled him, trying to keep him quiet. I connect with Bartimaeus's experience. Often, as I sense my need for God and begin to inwardly grope in his direction, a flood of voices assaults me, trying, it seems, to obstruct me from touching him.

These voices shout things like:

"It's no use, Joel. Your need is way beyond your ability to trust God. Better come up with a different solution."

"What a fool you are! Cry out all you want. Nobody is listening."

"Hold it right there, buddy! You have a lot of imperfections to fix before God will listen to you about this."

"Hurry it up, Joel! Wrap this thing up. Time is tight, and you've got a lot of other things to get to today."

When it's time to pray, the air around me can erupt with a thousand voices intent on clogging my ears and deflecting me from God. At times like these, I sometimes turn to a special spiritual practice for help. In this practice, I form in my mind certain mental pictures that aid in slicing through the barrage. These pictures gather up my thoughts and intentions, giving them a focus and vigor that help me push through the storm.

Let me mention an example or two.

When I am feeling particularly buffeted by spiritual and emotional crosscurrents during prayer, I sometimes imagine myself chopping wood (believe it or not!). There is, for me, something in the focus and energy of guiding that imaginary ax through those imaginary logs that coalesces my intention to slice through the barriers that separate me from God. Often, as the wood chips fly, so do the voices that harass me.

When quiet intimacy is my goal, there is another mental scene I sometimes call to mind. In it I open a door, step through, and enter a room in which the only persons present are my heavenly Father and me. In that room I don't say a word. I just sit, kneel, or lie silently in his company. He looks lovingly upon me and I him. In this quiet place, I eventually hold lightly before him any subjects of concern.

Much of my prayer life is without mental images. Yet, like pulling a special tool from the tool crib every once in a while to perform a special job, sometimes mental pictures can help our hearts and minds make their way into the presence of God.

CLEAN HANDS

Earlier we pondered the subject of responsiveness to God. Connected with this topic, though with a somewhat negative twist, is another subject that has a huge impact on our ability to hear God: sin. If there is a single habit that most contributes to an inability to sense God's whisperings in our lives, at the top of the list would be a knowing embrace of attitudes and activities that we know are devoid of God.

The life of Solomon always gives me a shiver. Early in his career, the Bible says, Solomon heard from God in an extraordinary way. "God gave Solomon wisdom and very great insight, and a breadth of understanding as measureless as the sand on the seashore" (1 Kings 4:29).

Toward the end of his career, however, we see a very different Solomon. One who seems nearly devoid of God: "The words of the Teacher [Solomon], son of David, king in Jerusalem: 'Meaningless! Meaningless!' says the Teacher. 'Utterly meaningless! Everything is meaningless'" (Ecclesiastes 1:1, 2).

By what path did Solomon move from point A to point B? While we don't know the entire story, the Bible's account of Solomon's swelling focus on his own pleasure speaks of an increasing fixation on a small, godless agenda: "I denied myself nothing my eyes desired; I refused my heart no pleasure" (Ecclesiastes 2:10).

Solomon's crushing final experience of purposelessness shows a narrowing down into himself to the point where he was no longer able to perceive God as meaningfully present. The constricting effects of sin desensitized Solomon to God's presence and reality.

As a boy, my brother climbed up on the kitchen stove one day in a criminal search for cookies in the cupboard above. Successful in his theft, on the way down he rested his hand on an electric burner still hot from cooking. Oh my! (I don't remember whether he ate the cookie. I hope so. It was dearly earned!) Interestingly, the pain gave way after a while to an insensitivity of the skin in the area burned.

The Bible speaks of those who practice sin as having consciences "seared as with a hot iron" (1 Timothy 4:2). Sin embraced has a searing effect on our sensitivity to God's voice.

THE BIBLE

In earlier chapters, we established that our key resource in listening to God is the Bible. The Bible plays a uniquely rich and textured melody about the one we worship. Listen often to that melody. Put yourself in its presence. Get to know its sounds, colors, and composition.

As your mind and heart repeatedly hear of Jesus Christ through the Scriptures, your spirit connects with the Holy Spirit and a deep resonance of spirits takes place (Romans 8:16). In this way God weaves himself into the very material of your soul. Such closeness and identification with God make it more and more natural to recognize his voice when he speaks.

NOT THE MESSAGE BUT THE VOICE

"The friend who attends the bridegroom waits and listens for him, and is full of joy when he hears the bridegroom's voice.

That joy is mine, and it is now complete. He must become greater; I must become less" (John 3:29, 30). What a wonderful final picture of listening for us to ponder! To what does the listener give attention? In what does the listener take delight? Attention rests in the bridegroom. Delight springs from the sound of his voice.

In the end, listening is not primarily about hearing. It is not about winning answers to questions or input on problems. Instead, listening is about the one heard. It is about attending to him, waiting on him, delighting in the sound of his foot on the path to our door. Listening to God is about rejoicing in his voice, whatever the message.

Dear Spirit of God, with a thousand distracting voices pressing for my attention, how do I hear such a quiet, patient voice as yours? No one has taught me this skill. Neither the world around me nor I seem made for it. But the times I catch your voice at home, in traffic, in conversations with my friends, through my Bible, in the beauty of your creation—it's at these times that my soul is most filled. Dear Holy Spirit, help me listen today beneath the busy surface of things for the voice that is real and true and will remain after all other competing voices have bowed in worship before it.

Amen.

9 WORSHIP

Treetops whizzed by beneath my feet. The winged stallion I found myself on was laboring hard. Terrified, it lunged forward in an effort to put distance between us and the four horsemen flying in pursuit. Dark and merciless, if they overtook us—I couldn't think of it.

But it was no good. With each moment, the distance between us decreased. In a few seconds, they would be on us. There was one chance. Maybe I could lose them in the thick clouds overhead. I jerked on the reigns and swept up into the hanging billow. Engulfed in the thick bank, we pushed up and up and up until suddenly, breaking above the cloud, I was met with a sight that put an instant end to all thought of the terror pursuing me.

Before me, spreading to the horizon and beyond, in every direction, stood a million angelic creatures—no—a *thousand million* radiant, otherworldly beings. Each on horseback, they sat in utter silence—motionless, without expression. Set forward at their front were a dozen sublime beings, also on winged horses. And ahead of them, a single commander, mounted on a trembling, magnificent charger. On earth, this charger would have been worshiped. In Heaven, it supported one much greater than itself.

The silence was arresting. Only the infrequent snorting or pawing of a nervous mount broke the quiet. I became like water poured out. No strength, no plan, no memory of anything that had taken place even a moment before. A sense of safety, but also of having stumbled with farmer's boots onto the stage of an exquisite, cosmic drama.

Mouth open, I gazed on this scene, when behind me, from below, my four pursuers suddenly burst through the clouds. They also instantly reigned up their mounts. But a moment later, with a scream of terror, they wheeled wildly around and plunged back into the clouds. The commander at the head of the legions motioned minutely with one finger, and ten horsemen broke rank, noiselessly hurtling past me and down through the clouds in pursuit.

I'm safe, I thought. *I'm home. It's over.*

A moment later, I woke up.

I lay for a long time in the darkness, riveted, pondering the place I had been visiting in the middle of the night. *A dream! Only a dream!* I thought. *Oh, that is just too, too bad!* I wanted to go back. If only in my dreams, I wanted to return to that place where a commander stands waiting, solving the universe by his presence. This is the treasure hidden in the field, the pearl of great price for which we will sell all we have. For this, giving thanks is not adequate. Even praise is not enough. This requires worship.

CREATED FOR WORSHIP

I have heard doubters say that human beings worship only because it makes them feel good. I doubt whether doubters have visited Heaven! They have not yet found themselves in that presence before whom the only possible response is worship—whether reluctantly or by desire. Believers grasp that human beings worship because we are built for it. There is something deep inside us, like a compass needle, that seeks out our spiritual true north, the object of our worship.

Human beings are always worshiping, at every moment. If we do not worship God, we will worship something else. If we do not adore the adored one, we will find some other thing upon which to spend our veneration. It may be as crude as abject personal pleasure or as apparently refined as beauty and truth.

But since our need for purpose is very high and our desire for a harmonizing focus must be constantly fed, we will always search for some object to adore as our master key, our solution to the puzzle of what it means to be alive.

And the thing we worship, we ultimately resemble. Some time ago, a woman shared with me that shortly after being married, her husband was shocked to discover her in the laundry room ironing her one-dollar bills. It was his first introduction to a subject that would provide many stimulating discussions in their marriage. There was just something this woman loved about money. She loved the feel of it, the look of it, and the heady sensation it gave when it was hers. But her life more and more resembled her money. Her personal value and sense of security were constantly negotiable, based on the numbers on the currency in her wallet.

It is this tendency to take up residency in the country of the thing we worship, to adopt its habits, customs, and personality, that puts worship at the head of God's top-ten list of commands. "I am the LORD your God, who brought you out of Egypt, out of the land of slavery. You shall have no other gods before me. You shall not make for yourself an idol in the form of anything in heaven above or on the earth beneath or in the waters below. You shall not bow down to them or worship them; for I, the LORD your God, am a jealous God" (Exodus 20:2-5).

As humans, it is inevitable that our hearts will search out lesser gods to worship. Our challenge as believers is to constantly slough off our homage to these little gods, who want to make us small like them. Our God, who has gone to great lengths in Christ to enlarge us into himself, is jealous that our hearts worship at only one throne.

This book is intended, in various ways, to encourage us to make all the ordinary activities of our lives arenas of worship. In this chapter, we focus on a particular kind of worship, the sort hinted at above the clouds in my dream. The type of worship we are allowed a peek into, here and there, throughout the Bible—moments when the holy expansiveness of God fills our consciousness and calls for our complete adoration.

THE ENGINE OF WORSHIP

What is it like for you to worship? What do you experience? What does your worship mean? I have sometimes wondered why I woke up from my dream at just the moment I did. I wonder if, perhaps, it was because I simply did not know what to do next. I had no experience, no point of reference for how one responds to the suffusing power and presence of God.

At the time of that dream (about thirty years ago), my practice of worship had a lot to do with making loud noises and feeling big feelings. I remember a time during my college days when a group of friends decided to get together one night to worship God. We found a small room in a busy campus building, closed the door, and went at it. Our exuberance was not appreciated by some who overheard us. I remember thinking, *Well, the godly in Christ shall suffer persecution.*

But later, on reflection, I decided that I agreed with our critics who suggested we weren't so much interested in worshiping God as worshiping worship. In such a frame of mind, had I stumbled into the hushed Heaven of my dream, I would have felt it my duty to stir things up, to get the place jumping. That approach to worship was not so much about my soul's delighted response to the presence of God as it was a formula of religious behavior rising out of my background and a yen for spiritual entertainment.

And this, it seems, points to a central purpose of worship. Worship does not seek an experience or a prescribed (and predictable) sequence of emotions and behaviors. Worship seeks God. Worship yearns, leans, cranes, listens for a commander. There is a throne at the center of the universe from which God reigns. Worship longingly feels its way there.

The Bible is full of images of those who followed their hearts into God's presence. One of my favorites, one we will visit several times in this chapter, is the story that the apostle John related about his friend Peter. Early one morning, shortly after Jesus' resurrection, the disciples were together in a boat, fishing. They had worked all night without success. Suddenly a man called to them from shore: "'Throw your net on the right side of the boat and you will find some.' When they did, they were unable to haul the net in because of the large number of fish" (John 21:6).

John peered hard at shore and exclaimed, "It's the Lord!" When Peter realized it was Jesus, he threw himself from the boat and began to swim toward shore. This image of Peter, leaping overboard, churning resolutely through the water in the direction of Jesus, is for me one of the thrilling pictures in the Gospels. Isn't this, perhaps, the first movement of the soul in worship? An intent longing to be at the side of Christ? An inner rush to eliminate the distance between us? Single-mindedness, disregard for obstacles, inattention to those who would oppose you—these, I think, propelled Peter.

Worship asks, "From where is Christ calling? How can my heart hurdle the distance? Let's go!"

An urge to draw tight to God's side wends its way throughout the whole Bible. Psalm 84 sighs: "My soul yearns, even faints, for the courts of the LORD; my heart and my flesh cry out for the living God. . . . Better is one day in your courts than a thousand elsewhere" (vv. 2, 10).

At lunchtime during summer Bible school, when I was about ten years old, I was playing with my friends when I noticed that my older brother, Kevin, was not with us. Searching the grounds did not turn him up. Hunting through the church and finally peering through the glass doors into the sanctuary, I discovered him sitting alone in a pew. *Whoa!* I thought. *Kevin got in trouble. They're making him sit in church during recess!* The only possibility I could imagine for sitting in a church sanctuary outside of the accepted requirements was as a penalty for some crime.

I stole up to his side.

"Pssst! What happened?" I asked.

Kevin slowly turned his bowed head toward me, then back to his business.

"Pssst! Kevin, what happened? Why are you here?"

"Nothing happened."

"Well, why are you here? What are you doing?"

"I'm just sitting here."

"What do you mean? Why are you sitting here? Don't you want to play? We're all playing."

"Yeah, I'll be out in a while."

"But why? What are you doing sitting here?"

My inquiries probably belonged in the category "If you have to ask the question, you won't understand the answer." Maybe Kevin didn't even know, at that moment, why he was attracted to that sanctuary, or what it was he was responding to. Even if he could have explained, I would not have understood at that time. Kevin was ahead of me. His nose had detected before mine the wafting aroma of that feast of which the psalmist hints: "One thing I ask of the LORD, this is what I seek: that I may dwell in the house of the LORD all the days of my life. . . . My heart says of you, 'Seek his face!' Your face, LORD, I will seek" (Psalm 27:4, 8).

In the grip of this desire, Peter rushed to shore. Emerging onto the beach, he stood dripping wet before Christ. With no plan or program beyond an intense yearning to be in Jesus' company, this unkempt Peter is to me an image of naked worship. Everything left behind. Responsibilities temporarily abandoned, handed to others to worry about. Maybe Peter's friends resented him a bit for deserting them to bring in the boat, heavy with the miraculous catch, without his help. Maybe they felt that Peter was acting selfishly, irresponsibly. Maybe they secretly sniffed at his unsophisticated behavior. For those not gripped by worship, the worshiper's motives are sometimes misunderstood.

THE VALUE OF WORSHIP

Maybe more often than worship's motives, it is worship's *value* that comes under fire. Worship doesn't seem to produce anything. It soaks up time with no identifiable result. It doesn't plant the crops, run the machinery, write the sermon, visit the sick, or achieve any other measurable outcome. Depending on your priorities, this can be terribly annoying.

As Jesus and his disciples were on their way, he came to a
village where a woman named Martha opened her home
to him. She had a sister called Mary, who sat at the Lord's
feet listening to what he said. But Martha was distracted by
all the preparations that had to be made. She came to him
and asked, "Lord, don't you care that my sister has left me
to do the work by myself? Tell her to help me!"

"Martha, Martha," the Lord answered, "you are
worried and upset about many things, but only one
thing is needed. Mary has chosen what is better, and it
will not be taken away from her" (Luke 10:38-42).

It is surprising to me that many today still cluck at Mary in
this passage for being spacey, unrealistic, maybe lazy—detached
from the real needs of the moment. I prefer Jesus' assessment.
Martha's heart at that moment, he observed, was "worried and
upset." Mary, on the other hand, releasing typical expectations,
had recognized and "chosen what is better." We must take Jesus
seriously about this. He knows. He sets the standard. Maybe he's
OK with getting less work done, or in doing more in a different
way. Whichever the case, with Jesus, there is a priority of worship
over work. Work is launched and empowered by worship but is
never a substitute for it.

Back on the beach, we are not allowed to observe the private few minutes Peter spent with Jesus before the other disciples joined them. Those few moments are frustratingly intriguing to me, like a locked cabinet or curtained stage. Maybe there are no words to express what passed between them. Peter's heart was likely full of his recent denial of Jesus, his doubts and questions about the future. Maybe he was embarrassed that Jesus found him so quickly reverting to his old occupation, fishing. Jesus would speak restoratively with Peter about these things very soon (John 21:15-17). But not now. This was not a moment for teaching or correction. This was a time for mutual love—a time for Jesus and Peter to enjoy each other's affection.

Peter's frailty opens a doorway for you and me into worship. Jesus calls us to join him at the fire, beside Peter, with all of our failures, recent denials, brash mistakes, and losses of faith. We are not to let our struggle with our imperfections rob us of worship. Our failures and messes, in fact, require the fire of worship in order to be purified, dissolved, and relieved.

The other disciples followed in the boat, towing the net full of fish, for they were not far from shore, about a hundred yards. When they landed, they saw a fire of burning coals there with fish on it, and some bread.

Jesus said to them, "Bring some of the fish you have just caught."

Simon Peter climbed aboard and dragged the net ashore. It was full of large fish, 153, but even with so many the net was not torn (John 21:8-11).

Jesus said, "Bring some of the fish you have just caught." The passage tells us that the disciples netted 153 fish. So many "they were unable to haul the net in because of the large number of fish" (v. 6). Yet the passage also indicates that, at Jesus' request, Peter jumped into the boat alone and dragged the net ashore. In this we witness a natural effect of worship. Worship creates a longing and energy to serve God. "Stand back! I'll do it. I'm on the job!"

This is where those who devalue worship as an unproductive drain of time have missed it. Worship inspires a longing to labor with Christ. Worship creates vision. It stirs a willingness to suffer the trials and pains of the work.

Mary's worship, for example, prepared her for a moment of ministry that Jesus said will be talked about until the end of time. Just days before his death—a death no one but Jesus was expecting—Jesus was at a dinner in his honor in the home of a man known as Simon the Leper (Matthew 26, John 12). Present were Lazarus, whom Jesus had recently raised from the dead; Lazarus's sisters, Mary and Martha; the disciples; a crowd; and likely some of Jesus' enemies. Each was preoccupied with his own important agenda: the disciples were probably still stewing about who among them was most important (Mark 9:33, 34); the crowd craned its neck to see the miracle man, Lazarus; and Jesus' enemies, resentful of his popularity, were perfecting their plans to kill him. In the midst of all this unenlightened busyness, only the worshipful Mary was in tune with the single thing called for.

Perhaps not entirely understanding her own actions, yet responding to God's Spirit, Mary anointed Jesus for his death. Others criticized her for being off base, but Jesus said, "Why are you bothering this woman? She has done a beautiful thing to me. . . . Wherever this gospel is preached throughout the world, what she has done will also be told, in memory of her" (Matthew 26:10, 13). Worship creates souls that sense the moment and minister in appropriateness and power.

The apostle Paul's ministry was also rooted in and directed by worship. Paul made clear that it was his personal, intimate vision of Christ that was the springboard for his entire ministry. Defending his mission before the Roman authorities, Paul said, "I was not disobedient to the vision from heaven" (Acts 26:19).

Paul's ministry resulted directly from his numerous encounters with heaven—his soul's deep acquaintance with Christ. "I want you to know, brothers," said Paul, "that the gospel I preached is not something that man made up. I did not receive it from any man, nor was I taught it; rather, I received it by revelation from Jesus Christ" (Galatians 1:11, 12).

What does this reveal to us of the secret of Paul's ministry, his vision and energy, his willingness to suffer for Christ at levels we cannot understand? (See 2 Corinthians 11:24-28.) Some have said that Paul would have been a great preacher to listen to on Sunday but a real pain to be around on Monday. Why? Because he was so focused on Christ that he never let up. He never turned it off. While I think the evidence shows that Paul may have been a little more diplomatic than that, you can see the point. Paul was intense. He had seen something; he had been there. He had made contact; he was a changed man. This is the effect of that personal vision of God experienced in worship.

THE NOURISHMENT OF WORSHIP

Having dragged the heavy load of fish ashore, Peter rejoined the group. "Jesus said to them, 'Come and have breakfast.' None of the disciples dared ask him, 'Who are you?' They knew it was the Lord" (John 21:12). The disciples, at that moment, did a wise thing. They listened to their inner knowing. "They knew it was the Lord." They did not question Jesus, probe him, make him prove his identity or reality. They trusted what they knew.

When we are with Jesus in worship, we also are wise if we rest in our knowing. In worship, one part of us wants to scurry around, sniffing out proofs for our experience. "Is this real? Is it truly God? Did I feel him right there? Are we really touching?" But Jesus said that his sheep know (John 10:4). Relax in that knowing. Spend your time during worship worshiping, not playing detective. Chances are, not all you feel during worship is God, as a matter of fact. But he is there, in and beyond your feelings, embracing your prostrate heart.

Resting in Jesus' presence, rather than scrutinizing the experience, prepared the disciples to receive much-needed nourishment.

"Jesus said to them, 'Come and have breakfast.' . . . Jesus came, took the bread and gave it to them, and did the same with the fish" (John 21:12, 13). This, finally, is the chief gift of worship: worship feeds us.

My interrupted audience with Jesus Christ, gifted to me as a dream many years ago, has nourished me ever since. At the time, I went in the strength of it for many days. Gradually, it became a reminder of where my fulcrum lay, the supernatural central pivot around which the rest of my life would turn. "You have come to God, the judge of all men, to the spirits of righteous men made perfect, to Jesus the mediator of a new covenant" (Hebrews 12:23, 24).

I like to imagine that among the heavenly host of my dream, set back a respectful distance from his commander, was the spirit of a righteous man, newly arrived by Heaven's standards. A. W. Tozer had recently left these words to the church on earth:

The world is perishing for lack of the knowledge of God, and the Church is famishing for want of His presence. The instant cure of most of our religious ills would be to enter the Presence . . . , to become suddenly aware that we are in God and God is in us. This would lift us out of our pitiful narrowness and cause our hearts to be enlarged. . . . To penetrate, to push in sensitive living experience into the holy Presence, is a privilege open to every child of God.[1]

Jesus called out to them, "Come and have breakfast."

Baggy-eyed and empty-handed, unsure about their future, each alone in his most private thoughts and needs, "they saw a fire of burning coals there with fish on it, and some bread. . . . Jesus came, took the bread and gave it to them, and did the same with the fish" (John 21:9, 13).

Come.

From what far shore is Jesus calling you? Through what lifting fog have you begun to hear his voice? Fling yourself from your isolated boat. Feel your way in his direction. Respond to Jesus' banquet offer: "Come worship. Come dine. Meat and fish, bread and wine. Springs of eternal water bubbling up from within. Warmth and light from my mending fire to comfort your aching soul."

I turned around to see . . . someone "like a son of man," dressed in a robe reaching down to his feet and with a golden sash around his chest. His head and hair were white like wool, as white as snow, and his eyes were like blazing fire. His feet were like bronze glowing in a furnace, and his voice was like the sound of rushing waters. In his right hand he held seven stars, and out of his mouth came a sharp double-edged sword. His face was like the sun shining in all its brilliance.

When I saw him, I fell at his feet as though dead. Then he placed his right hand on me and said: "Do not be afraid. I am the First and the Last. I am the Living One; I was dead, and behold I am alive for ever and ever! And I hold the keys of death and Hades." . . .

Then I looked and heard the voice of many angels, numbering thousands upon thousands, and ten thousand times ten thousand. They encircled the throne and the living creatures and the elders. In a loud voice they sang:

"Worthy is the Lamb, who was slain, to receive

power and wealth and wisdom and strength and honor
and glory and praise!"

Then I heard every creature in heaven and on earth
and under the earth and on the sea, and all that is in
them, singing:

"To him who sits on the throne and to the Lamb
be praise and honor and glory and power, for ever and
ever!" (Revelation 1:12-18; 5:11-13).

Amen.

Dear Jesus, like Peter, my heart has so often felt at sea, as though alone in a dark night—laboring, cold, and hungry. But lately, Lord, you are becoming company to me, offering warmth, nourishment, and light. I thought you were far away, but now I see you are nearby. I thought the dark night ruled, but now I know that you rule without rival and without contradiction. All my seas of hopelessness and seasons of lonely labor I lay down at your fire. Cure what can be cured, Lord. Burn up what must be destroyed. Only let me stay before you and cry, "Honor and glory and power to the Son, the Living One, for ever and ever!"

Amen.

RELISHING HIS PURPOSE

My food is to do the will of him who sent me.

John 4:34

10 PURPOSE

In Minnesota, where I live, Sven and Ole jokes are a gentle way to poke some fun at a frozen northern-European way of doing life. I heard this one recently: It seems Ole was shipwrecked alone on a desert island. Since he was a handy guy and had plenty of time on his hands, he decided to build himself a town. When he was finally rescued, he gave his rescuers a tour of his personal village. "Yah, over der is de library," Ole said, "and next to dat is de community center. And over der is de church I go to, yust across de street from de church I used to go to."

Hmmm. I guess Ole had an argument with himself at his former church that couldn't be resolved. Naturally, there was nothing left to do but shake the dust from his feet and start something new. Sort of funny—in a sort of familiar way.

Is the joke's implication about Christians true? What are our core values? Are squabbles and loud opinions and a tendency to complain about the management the things that most characterize us? As Christians, what turns us on, motivates us, preoccupies us? Where is our best energy invested?

GOD'S PRIORITY LIST

Look, for a moment, at the list below. On a scale of one through four, with one being most important and four being least important, how would you rank the items based on the time and energy Christians give to each?

- Intimacy with God
- Behavior
- Serving others
- Beliefs

I don't know how the list strikes you, but when I have asked this question of small groups during classes or retreats, invariably it shakes out like this:

1. Behavior
2. Beliefs

3. Serving others

4. Intimacy with God

It seems that mandating and monitoring correct ways to act and think have emerged over the years as the chief pastime of the Christian faith. Such an emphasis leads to the tense, self-conscious, comparing style of religion that, for too many, has become synonymous with Christianity. The only upside I can think of to this approach to faith is that it sometimes produces a good Sven and Ole joke!

I was intrigued, some years ago, by a television interview of a comedian well known for lampooning religious figures. He had just finished writing and starring in a movie set in Palestine at the time of Christ that took an irreverent approach to topics most of us would consider sacred. The comedian said that he found it easy to make fun of religious people in the movie but had a hard time making fun of Jesus Christ. There was no end to the humorous insults that could be invented about Christians, he said, but Christ himself would just not be funny! Why? To make fun of religion, he observed, you have to find something base to ridicule—hypocrisy, for example, or greed, pretense, shallowness, prejudice, and so on. In religious people, this man noted, there is no end to these things. But you can't find them in Jesus, so he's not funny.

As I pondered these comments, I thought, *You know, I don't recall ever hearing a Mother Teresa joke. And I don't think I've ever heard a Billy Graham joke. Among all the funny stories that skewer religion, I have never heard these two believers lampooned.* Then it occurred to me: what would you make fun of? Their integrity? Their self-sacrifice? Their habit of loving and living for others?

There are some among us, it appears, who have gotten it, some who have figured out a way to give blood and breath and bone to the words of the Bible. On these believers, Jesus' words rest comfortably: "By this all men will know that you are my disciples, if you love one another" (John 13:35).

Wouldn't it be great to be known for that kind of love? Wouldn't it be wonderful at work, at home, in our community, or in whatever circles we frequent to be identified like that? "Oh yes," people would say, "she's a little unusual with her obsession with God and everything, but talk about loving! Talk about giving herself for others! There is something incredible about her. People like that could almost make you believe there is a God."

Let's revisit that list above. Rate the items once more. Only this time, rate them according to the priority you think God probably gives each one. Which would you guess is most important to him, next most important, and so on? If your results are like those of the small groups I have surveyed, you will notice that God's order of priority is precisely opposite of ours:

(1) Intimacy with God

2. Serving others

3. Beliefs

4. Behavior

God's focus is intimacy first, out of which arises a natural desire to love and serve others. Beliefs and behavior, though important, follow. Such a picture of the purpose of life is spoken to in these wonderful lines from the book of Matthew:

> One of them, an expert in the law, tested him with this question: "Teacher, which is the greatest commandment in the Law?"
>
> Jesus replied: "'Love the Lord your God with all your heart and with all your soul and with all your mind.' This is the first and greatest commandment. And the second is like it: 'Love your neighbor as yourself.' All the Law and the Prophets hang on these two commandments" (Matthew 22:35-40).

So far this book has given much emphasis to the first half of Jesus' equation in these verses—loving God with our whole heart, soul, and mind. The next few chapters will ponder the result that, according to Jesus, naturally follows—a growing love for and service extended to those around us. In this chapter, we will give some thought to the question of loving service as the Christian's fundamental purpose in the world. In the next two chapters, we will tackle some of the issues that emerge when we think about pursuing this purpose, in particular "What is my specific calling, and how do I discern it among the many good possibilities?"

INVISIBLE SERVANTS

Earlier I alluded to Billy Graham and Mother Teresa as models of those who have responded to God's call to love others with the love they first received from Christ. To only speak of well-known people like that, however, would be elitist, as though the only ones who live that way are famous, on a different plane than the rest of us. In fact, those who make it their special purpose to serve are often right next to us—though nearly invisible. Their meekness and focus on others make them tend to disappear.

Think for a moment: are you connected, in any way, to someone whose tendency and direction in life always seems to lean toward loving, embracing, and serving others? Anybody whose daily schedule seems a little careless of the responsibilities that usually rule life, giving him or her time and energy for others? It could be a relative or a friend or someone in your church or across the street. Most of us know one or two of these quiet folks whose lives are flavored by and intent on loving outreach. My friend Frank fits this description.

Frank works in the graphic arts world. He is very talented, creating layouts for promotional catalogues and business advertisements. Fifteen years ago, the alternating pieces that formed the purpose of his life were a new house, the advancement of his career, his hobbies, and his family. But a series of encounters with Jesus began to form some new thinking inside him.

Regarding his job, for example, Frank began to understand things differently than in the past. While before his career had primarily been a delivery system for personal advancement, perks, and cash, gradually he began to understand it as a platform for touching others' lives. Surrounded by men and women like himself—hungry, seeking purpose, sometimes in pain—Frank began to see his workplace as an arena to minister Christ. In fact, Frank turned down a couple of promotions in order to honor a growing sense of call to be a presence of hope to his fellow workers in the trenches.

To free up time to spend with others who also wanted a new way of living, Frank pulled back from the overtime he had been in the habit of working—the overtime he had needed to pay for his big new house. He and his wife decided to trade that home for a more modest one. He even sold his pricey car in preference for something more economical. Gradually his life took a shape that supported his new emphasis on helping birth God's life in others.

There are some disadvantages to Frank's new plan for life. He isn't the one thought of today when the vice presidents of his company are looking for somebody to round out a foursome at the golf course. And his name is no longer put forward when they are considering someone to promote. On the other hand, when a co-worker's marriage is collapsing or a child is in trouble, Frank's phone is the one that rings. His co-workers don't quite get Frank, but they are glad he is around when life's hard issues come knocking.

Those who make others their primary focus in life might, like Frank, be considered a little odd. They are sometimes dismissed as unrealistic, not in tune with reality, even lazy. Their preoccupation with the hidden things of God leads them to mystify friends and relatives who see them let opportunities go by that our culture has identified as central to life's purpose—chances to make more money, advance their careers, or in other ways firm up their personal kingdoms. They are countercultural. Their most prized work—God's grace taking root in others' lives—is devalued by a society that rates purpose quite differently. They are marginalized as eccentric, or maybe as going through a phase that hopefully will pass. They are not often the movers and shakers, even in the churches they attend, content as they are to do small, quiet things that minister Christ to their brethren. They are ones who have found a home in sentiments like these from Paul:

> Therefore, I urge you, brothers, in view of God's mercy, to offer your bodies as living sacrifices, holy and pleasing to God—this is your spiritual act of worship. Do not conform any longer to the pattern of this world, but be transformed by the renewing of your mind. Then you will be able to test and approve what God's will is—his good, pleasing and perfect will (Romans 12:1, 2).

To fill the role illustrated in the verses above, we typically set certain individuals apart. We make a special class out of them. We pay them just enough to keep the wolves at bay and call them pastors or missionaries or Christian workers. But the Bible seems to invite each of us into this new work of God's kingdom.

SQUEEZED

"You are the light of the world. A city on a hill cannot be hidden. Neither do people light a lamp and put it under a bowl.

Instead they put it on its stand, and it gives light to everyone in the house. In the same way, let your light shine before men, that they may see your good deeds and praise your Father in heaven" (Matthew 5:14-16). Most of us really do want to let our lights shine. Having walked with God for a while, we have gained an appreciation for the gift we have been given, and we want, more and more, to find ways to share this with others in word and deed. The real challenge is not our desire but our schedule! In lives already overwhelmingly full of pressing projects, responsibilities, and the stern task of just trying to survive, it can feel nearly impossible to squeeze out any extra bits of time to reach out to others.

If your desire to serve God and others, on the one hand, bumps up against an unyielding schedule of necessary and competing activities on the other, what do you do? Let's explore a few issues that seem to have great bearing on the subject. The first begins with—a game of Monopoly!

Press delete

I know a guy we'll call Axel. All his life, Axel has been very competitive. In whatever situation he finds himself, Axel's main goal is to win. One blustery winter day, when he was about ten years old, Axel was playing a game of Monopoly with his brother. In the corner of the cozy living room where they sat crackled a cheery fire. As the game progressed, it began to look bad for Axel. He was losing houses and hotels left and right. A moment came when it became clear that there was no way he could win. In that instant, Axel rose with a glare, jerked the Monopoly board from the table, and flung the whole game into the fire!

Well, that's one way out of jail. Have you ever played a game like that—card games, board games, or athletic contests—and found yourself in the middle of what is essentially a meaningless competition, allowing it to take on an importance out of all proportion with reality? It just feels so significant. "My soul for Indiana Avenue!" It really seems necessary to win!

Sometimes it seems I've lived my life like a Monopoly game, allowing things ultimately unimportant to become my emotional focus. Projects, goals, and objectives that have little intrinsic value have soaked up my best energy.

"If we don't get this ratty hallway carpet replaced, the world is going to explode!"

"I'm going to beat my sales quota this year if it kills me. If I don't join the Million Dollar Club, thereby qualifying for the elite President's Cruise to Hawaii, I am going to die!"

"No, honey! You don't understand! We have got to schedule a vacation now, or we're going to lose our free air miles!"

"I vow, by the power of the gods, that I will be dandelion free this summer! Dandelion free, I tell you!!"

And so on. Sometimes we need to step back from the game and get some perspective. Sometimes we need to reanchor ourselves in the things God has truly given us to do and release the rest.

Over a period of ten years—and it took ten years—I let fall away more than half the activities that used to absorb my time and energy. I came to realize that they were motivated by desires and fears having more to do with my own insecurities and others' expectations than with God's interests. This has been a slow, experimental, sometimes hesitating exchange, but at length wonderfully freeing. So the first question is "How truly necessary are all the urgent activities and commitments that currently push and pull our lives?" <u>For which of them would God be in support of pressing the delete key</u>?

Look close at hand

A second observation is that God may not be so much interested in having us squeeze extra pieces of service into our lives as he is in transforming the tone and focus of the activities and relationships we already have. Remember Frank? When he was awakened to a new love for Christ, God could have laid on Frank all sorts of exotic assignments for service. But why do that? Frank was already connected with a host of people— friends, family, co-workers—who knew and trusted him. All of a sudden, God could love these people through Frank.

On being awakened by God, the question becomes "What are my present relationships about?" While before, the people in my life seemed there to further my interests, to serve me or entertain me, now I see myself as the servant of God's grace growing in them. That purpose sometimes demands big blocks of time. Yet just as often, it simply involves a new way of being present in my relationships with people—a new interest in their well-being, a supportive tone to my thoughts about them, a prayerful concern for their hidden world. This is not easy, of course. It requires saying no to the self-serving, utilitarian approach to relationships we are used to living. It means listening not only to others' words but to their lives. It means living availably. Yet it often also means living and serving right where we are, in the midst of the natural connections and relationships we already have.

Give yourself permission

Finally, when pursuing our desire to serve, we may need to give ourselves permission to live outside the ordinary patterns of life that our culture typically encourages. I think about Shari. A single woman in her forties, Shari feels called to volunteer in the service of seniors in the small community where she lives. She visits with them, helps them shop, takes them to the doctor, and much more. Her bits of service often fall during those hours when most of the rest of us are earning our living. To support her habit, Shari cleans homes and businesses during odd hours, earning enough to get along.

Or I think of Joel and Kathy. As an artist near the shores of Lake Superior, Joel understands his art as his service to God. While he could at any moment use his skills to make lots of money producing art that is more commercial, Joel is committed to painting and selling what God has given him. A remarkably simple lifestyle and a wife who buys into the value of living out one's purpose in Christ have enabled them to stay true to their calling. And Joel and Kathy's modeling of these values is producing children who are growing up to live the same way.

Oswald Chambers said one of the most difficult things to explain to others is God's call upon your life.[1] The call to service that feels so compelling to you is often met by others with a yawn. This lack of resonance and support sometimes adds to our reluctance to experiment in response to that quiet call. But if you look, you'll notice that those who serve often disregard the usual patterns that keep life safe, but boring. Protected, but sterile. Secure, but unfulfilling.

Glance, for example, through Hebrews 11. Ponder the lives of those mentioned in the Bible's "Hall of Faith." They are a fairly motley crew—out of the mainstream to be sure. They are pilgrims whose heavenly call urged them to leap beyond accepted boundaries in their service to God. And theirs is not such a bad result, is it? Haven't they been identified by God for all time as demonstrating to the world how to live life? We will be happy and wise if we catch the vision that they and Frank and Shari and Joel and Kathy and all the invisible servants around us have discovered, who each day quietly walk in life's richer purpose, to the delight of God.

Living out our purpose in God—our general purpose as loving servants and the specific purpose for which God has uniquely called and equipped us—is absolutely central to an experience of intimacy with God. Upon our purpose rests God's touch to inspire, empower, and lift us up. Within our purpose, we find we no longer live against the grain but begin to move and flow and have our being as children of God have been designed.

So what are the general outlines of this life purpose to which Christ calls us? What are its contours and shapes? What values are involved? What exactly is the believer's mission?

In the next two chapters, we will address more of the challenges of living out our mission in Christ and identify ways to uncover our particular calling within it.

Dear Father, I thank you for your wisdom deep inside me that won't let me rest satisfied in a purpose not worthy of your child. Give me eyes to see where substitute purposes have gripped me and the courage to grasp your offer of freedom. Help me desire, more and more, to be the servant of your grace working in my family, friends, co-workers, and all to whom you send me. Make my heart like your Son, in whose purpose I have come to life and whose servant-partner I am in loving, caring for, and reconciling this world to you.

Amen.

11 CALLING

Spuds MacKenzie. Remember the name?

Spuds was a dog, a bull terrier. Some years ago, he was the mascot for a national beer company. As the marketing vehicle for his product, the advertisers gave Spuds the aura of being human. They dressed him in a coat and tails, put a beverage in his hand, surrounded him with admirers, photographed him in racy cars, posed him in a beach chair by the ocean, and in other ways made Spuds look hip.

While watching a Spuds commercial one day, my daughter, Monica, about ten years old at the time, sighed, "I feel sorry for Spuds. They shouldn't make him do those things. They should let him go outside and run and play and be with his dog friends." To this, my son David, barely six, immediately responded, "Well, Monica, after all, they *have* made him the richest dog in America!"

In parenting, one of the hardest parts of the job is to wait to laugh until later. What a hilarious remark! Yet it was not only funny but, for me, thick with meaning. I wondered, *Where did my six-year-old son already learn that it's OK to do the things in life you are not designed to do as long as somebody pays you enough money to do them? Is the idea of selling our fundamental identity for meager compensations so heavily in the air that even a little boy assumes that this is the economy of life?* Very funny comment. Very disturbing.

Our personal invitation from God to live a life that expresses our individual calling is one of the most precious gifts of heaven. A tendency to trade it for substitute favors is alarming and sad. There is an organic connection between living out our calling and walking intimately with God because our calling so fits our individual design. It suits the longings we feel and allows release of deep urges in need of expression. Responding to our calling tends to lead us down pathways pregnant with experiences that God plans to use to challenge, amaze, and inspire us into deeper things in him.

In the previous chapter, we discovered that the Christian's general purpose in this world is to love God intimately and, out of this love, to give himself to the caring ministry of God's grace in the people and world around him. In this chapter and the next, we ask a further question: "Within this general purpose, what are the specific ways I am invited to live it out? To what activities am I personally called? For what relationships, duties, and vocation am I uniquely equipped?"

Our individual call may express itself in a wide variety of ways: in volunteer activities, our current work and relationships, a specific vocational setting, or some combination of these. Calling is unique. There are no formulas or rules. Living out your calling does not make life easier but lends it a certain sense of rightness that human beings deeply crave. Pursuing our calling creates many questions but addresses the Big Question— what am I on this earth to do?

But let's take a half-step backwards. Before launching out on a chapter devoted to extolling the virtues of personal calling, let me say something that may seem to cut against where we have been going so far. It is this: discovering and living out your own special life calling, while important, is not essential to your well-being in Christ. That's right. Your fundamental welfare, deepest happiness, and experience of intimacy with God will not be held hostage when circumstances don't allow you to fully engage the life you are best designed to live. Remember, across history many believers have been prevented from living out their gifts and calling—women, slaves, the uneducated, the poor.

If your own life circumstances deprive you of the liberty to fully walk out your calling in Christ, are you marooned to a subpar experience of God? On the contrary. Times of fellowship with the one you love are more precious in prison than on the outside. And fellowship with God amidst the sufferings of a life imprisoned by circumstances beyond our control can also be intimately sweet. What circumstances do I have in mind? Some of us are in relationships that obstruct our calling. Others face financial or physical limitations. Some are in awkward stages of life or have not had access to necessary training. A wide variety of past choices and current dilemmas can put the calling we yearn to live frustratingly beyond reach.

Let's begin this chapter by balancing the concept of calling with a more profound one—grace. Grace extended, first of all, to ourselves in whatever situation we find ourselves. While this book will hopefully stir up our desire to discover and live out our unique life purpose in God, still, we Christians are people who "have learned to be content whatever the circumstances" (Philippians 4:11). We do not find our deepest purpose in purpose but in Jesus himself.

CALLED BEYOND CONFINEMENT

More important to our relationship with Christ than living out a particular calling is an attitude of humble availability. Is it our desire that our lives would be extravagantly available to God for his purposes, whatever they may be? Whether those purposes involve living the calling for which we have been gifted or mysteriously entail confinement in circumstances counterproductive to it? The apostle Paul, whose call to preach the gospel was often hemmed in and dammed up by his repeated persecutions and imprisonments, rested in a deeper purpose in the midst of his captivity.

"We are hard pressed on every side, but not crushed; perplexed, but not in despair; persecuted, but not abandoned; struck down, but not destroyed. We always carry around in our body the death of Jesus, so that the life of Jesus may also be revealed" (2 Corinthians 4:8-10).

Paul fed his heart upon Jesus himself. He recognized and accepted the tension between the purpose and direction inside him and his inability in this present life to express it all (Romans 8:22, 23). Paul's confidence is deep that our fundamental well-being cannot be moved by circumstances that sometimes restrict us. "We know," he says, "that in all things God works for the good of those who love him, who have been called according to his purpose. . . . Who shall separate us from the love of Christ? Shall trouble or hardship or persecution or famine or nakedness or danger or sword?" (vv. 28, 35). What about a calling short-circuited by a lack of education or an unsupportive spouse or want of opportunity or shortage of money or interfering responsibilities or physical restrictions? "No," says Paul, "in all these things we are more than conquerors through him who loved us" (v. 37).

The purposes God intends for our lives are not limited to this lifetime but extend into eternity. Many believe that the unique passions, skills, and gifts God has placed in us will only find their complete fulfillment in Heaven, where God will continue to develop them for his glory forever. God will not be frustrated in his plans for us.

DISCERNING OUR CALL

Though pursuing the unique service in Christ for which we are designed is sometimes not possible (or not possible right now), on the other hand, particularly in today's Western cultures, it often is. Challenging, but within reach. Requiring sacrifice, but attainable.

How do we start?

First, recall again Jesus' great command to loving service noted in the last chapter: "Love your neighbor as yourself" (Matthew 22:39). The New Testament unpacks these words in many passages that help illustrate what this love looks like and what you and I look like when we're doing it. Four main characteristics come to mind:

Christians love others:

• as servants (Mark 9:33-35)

• as uniquely gifted (1 Peter 4:10)

• as reconcilers (2 Corinthians 5:17-20)

• as worshipers (Romans 12:1-8; 1 Peter 4:11)

When we synthesize Jesus' great command to love (Matthew 22:35-40) with these descriptive characteristics, we can write a general life-purpose statement that might look something like this: *My purpose in Christ is to love God with all my heart and to express worship in using my gifts to serve others, calling them to reconciliation with God.*

Such a statement is helpful in that it begins to define the playing field, but it still leaves me with the pressing question "What is my particular position in the game?" How do I get in touch with that unique way of expressing Christ that God has in mind for me? The Bible indicates that all Christians have the responsibility to probe the possibilities of their unique call despite the obstacles and risks (Matthew 25:14-30). And there are obstacles! As I have spoken with others about the subject over the years, some common hurdles have emerged that many face who pursue God's call.

Time

Discovering and developing our calling takes time. With time in such chronically short supply all around, investing the thought, prayer, and action needed to pursue our calling in Christ requires a deliberate, persistent choice of will.

Unawareness of the possibilities

To some, the thought that God has a special calling in mind for their lives is a new idea—intriguing, puzzling, maybe a little intimidating. Until the possibility of a unique call dawns, we tend to give our lives to the best options we can engineer, usually in line with the accepted values of the culture.

Lack of permission

Some of us feel a definite sense of direction but lack the emotional permission to pursue it. We feel "I'm not allowed. Other people can embrace their calling, but not me." To some, the calling they sense doesn't seem important or "spiritual" enough, so they discount it. Others see the risks involved, and though wanting to take a shot at it, they feel, on some deep level, that this may be an irresponsible quest.

Others question their own motives or interpret taking steps in pursuit of their calling as self-promotion. Some are waiting for an unmistakable supernatural sign of God's approval. Others interpret roadblocks and difficulties as God's disapproval. A lack of emotional permission to live out our calling and giftedness is a big barrier to life purpose.

- *Fear of failure and the unknown*

A friend recently shared about a particular life call of which he is aware. But fearing that he may make mistakes along the way, he has not been willing to put his toe on the path. With the subject of calling, the stakes feel high, and the fear of making a mistake can pinch off the process before it starts.

- *Money*

For those whose calling impacts their vocation, the question of money often looms. Sometimes the question is how to support oneself in response to God's call. Sometimes the issue is one of willingness to accept a reduced lifestyle. Either way, money is a challenge.

Disapproval

A friend who feels called to visit the elderly in nursing homes says that sometimes the simple prospect of her husband's disapproval of this use of her time keeps her home. The tendency of others to question, disapprove, or discount our call may create confusion in us and a tendency to stay put.

Incompatible desires

Our divided desires sometimes torpedo our pursuit of calling. We all experience a desire for security, leisure, and material things—in themselves all good. But sometimes too much of a good thing can become the enemy of the best.

KICKING THE STICKS

For all the challenges involved, however, the urge to respond to our own special leading is very strong. In the life of the apostle Paul, Scripture offers us some unique insights about discerning and living out our call.

Paul gives comfort to those of us who sometimes feel in the dark regarding our usefulness and call. Because of his larger-than-life role in the birth of the Christian church, it is hard to grasp how out of touch Paul was, at one time, regarding his own call. But Paul was desperately out of touch! In fact, when God first burst through to him, Paul was steaming with violent intent toward the young Christian church in the city of Damascus, bent on a program of persecution. As he approached the city, however, in a pure gift from heaven, Paul experienced a vision that he relates in Acts 26:14, 15: "We all fell to the ground, and I heard a voice saying to me in Aramaic, 'Saul, Saul, why do you persecute me? It is hard for you to kick against the goads.' Then I asked, 'Who are you, Lord?' 'I am Jesus, whom you are persecuting,' the Lord replied."

There is a particular phrase I would like to highlight from the passage. Jesus said, "Saul, . . . it is hard for you to kick against the goads" (v. 14). Ouch! Yes. It hurts to kick against goads. Goads (for us city kids) are the sharp sticks used to prick oxen to compel them to continue pulling in their furrows. Paul's life, at this moment, was a constant mutiny against God's prodding. Paul's first order of business in discerning his future was to stop kicking against the goads and yield himself to God. Discernment of our call begins with yielding.

What do we need to yield? Maybe our desire for a particular future. Maybe a preference for one sort of calling over another. Maybe a demand for safety and smooth sailing ahead. I don't know. But yielding into God's care our plans, hopes, desires, and personal preferences is a necessary doorway through which we must pass on our way to discovering our calling. George Mueller, himself an astute listener to God's voice, once observed, "Nine-tenths of the difficulties are overcome when our hearts are ready to do the Lord's will, whatever it may be. When one is truly in this state, it is usually but a little way to the knowledge of what His will is."[1]

LOOK UP

For years my friend Sue had mulled the question of God's call upon her life. She had attended self-discovery seminars, taken the popular gifts and talents tests, and counseled with pastors and vocational experts, but she continued confused and a little

Soul Craving

depressed. She discovered many options that were not a good fit but could not identify a calling that seemed her own. With the apparent failure of every avenue of discovery, Sue began to cry out to God with a pained sense of urgency and near despair.

One day during a church service, quite apart from anything the pastor was saying, an inner impression came upon Sue so strongly that she nearly turned to see who had spoken. In that moment, in a message of just a few words, a sense of calling coalesced inside her that gathered up Sue's core passions and focused them in a suddenly obvious direction. The direction seemed so natural and so consistent with how she was wired that Sue broke into a smile and heard herself whisper a half-embarrassed "Duh!"

The apostle Paul's life also teaches us that apart from the many valuable self-discovery tools and techniques available today for discerning calling—some of which we will discuss soon—our primary focus of inquiry should be God himself.

"I want you to know, brothers, that the gospel I preached is not something that man made up. I did not receive it from any man, nor was I taught it; rather, I received it by revelation from Jesus Christ" (Galatians 1:11, 12).

Shortly after Jesus bumped Paul to the ground on the Damascus road, Paul retreated—some scholars believe for as much as three years—to the deserts of Arabia to inquire of God regarding this new thing that had been born inside him (Galatians

1:15-17). During this time of attentiveness, Paul received insights and personal direction from Christ that cemented his understanding of his call (2 Corinthians 12:1-6; Ephesians 3:1-9). The result was a permeating sense of personal assignment that made Paul's calling clear and gave him the passion he needed to bear the suffering that would accompany it.

Discerning our call to service in Christ is not just a mechanical affair, one that can be precisely identified through self-study, counseling, surveys, and tools. Beyond those, there is mystery involved—a deeply unique seizing of our passion and imagination rising from a personal vision of Christ. Let's allow Paul's and Sue's experiences to instruct us in this. Personal and sometimes desperate inquiry of God leads to inner vision. This vision conveys power. It holds surprises. It is more pregnant and wonderful than the thing we dream up ourselves. Vision from God cannot be controlled and is on a timetable all its own. Our role is primarily to cast our eyes and hearts patiently upward.

The idea of fixing our attention above makes me think of my old dog and pal, Rocky. Often while I read a book or watched television, Rocky rested at my feet. Sometimes when I got up to go to the kitchen, Rocky was actually up a moment before me, leading the way. I wondered, *How does he do that?* Then I realized that he had been watching me even when I wasn't paying any attention to him. He had been waiting upon me, sensing my mood, anticipating my interests. Maybe that's a good model for discerning God's direction for us. Alertness, patience, availability, worship, and love. If we don't prefer such a panting, attentive relationship with God, it may be hard to discover the direction he is heading.

THIS LITTLE JEWEL

Paul was terribly grateful for the mission God entrusted to him. "I thank Christ Jesus our Lord," he said, ". . . that he considered me faithful, appointing me to his service" (1 Timothy 1:12). Paul knew his mission and liked it. He received it as a special favor from God. His example is permission for some of us and a command for others: value, honor, and embrace your uniqueness and calling! I personally struggled awhile before accepting my own particular gifts and calling in Christ.

The works of the remarkable English writer C. S. Lewis have been important to me. Some years ago, I read a biography of Lewis that described his weekly meetings with a group of writers and intellectuals who called themselves The Inklings. As I read about the rarified atmosphere of conversation and debate that attended those meetings, I found myself strangely depressed. It was some time before I understood why. It turns out I was downhearted because it had become clear, in observing the interactions of these brilliant men, that my own abilities would never operate on their level. Somehow, the sort of talk they enjoyed and the vocations they lived seemed very important to me. Now, plainly aware that I would never stroll those deep forests, I was bummed. For some months, and at one level for years afterward, I inwardly fingered a disgust at my own small abilities, a frustration with God for allowing me to view that pleasant country but not live there, and a dejected envy for a fruitfulness I craved but could never achieve. (My pride and insecurity in this, as you might notice, run very deep.)

However, over many years my perspective has shifted. While at some level the pangs of my preferences still waft in the air, I have found great joy in learning to embrace the person I am, as someone God has made especially for himself. I have exchanged a fixation on my own abilities for a focus on our shared love. It has been a great weight lifted from me to no longer hanker after things I am not built for or intended to do. My unique individuality has become my treasured home; my personal, little assignment from God my jewel to place upon my bridegroom's finger.

Paul's conviction about the value of our uniqueness in God becomes an invitation for everyone in the body of Christ: "Now the body is not made up of one part but of many. . . . If the whole body were an eye, where would the sense of hearing be? If the whole body were an ear, where would the sense of smell be? But in fact God has arranged the parts in the body, every one of them, just as he wanted them to be. If they were all one part, where would the body be?" (1 Corinthians 12:14, 17-19).

MY ASSIGNED DUTY

As I began to embrace the value of my particular gifts, there came a time, after much prayer, self-discovery, counsel, and confirmation, when I had developed quite a good understanding of my calling. Then another wrinkle appeared—a doubt. *Yes, I thought, it is a good call. In fact it is the very thing I want to do and feel most equipped to do. But, I began to wonder, is it the very best thing I could do? Is there not, perhaps, some bit of service more valuable to God, more effective, more needed at this time in his world?* And so I wavered, for a time, to fully respond to God in my unique, revealed calling.

Somehow, though, God made it clear that my individual call does not have to answer every need, just the particular one to which I have been assigned duty. "There are different kinds of gifts, but the same Spirit. There are different kinds of service, but the same Lord. There are different kinds of working, but the same God works all of them in all men" (1 Corinthians 12:4-6).

So, our uniqueness is precious, and the way we value it is first by working to uncover it and then by embracing what we find. A culture that urges conformity (often in pursuit of security) has made our job harder. But these days there are many wonderful self-discovery tools that can help us clear away the debris disguising our identity. In the next chapter, we will explore several activities that can help us get a fix on our uniqueness and calling in Christ.

ISLANDS OF LIGHT

One day, at a time when Paul's own unique call was still gestating inside him, he found himself worshiping God with a group of his friends. "While they were worshiping the Lord and fasting, the Holy Spirit said, 'Set apart for me Barnabas and Saul for the work to which I have called them.' So after they had fasted and prayed, they placed their hands on them and sent them off" (Acts 13:2, 3).

Wow! That was quick. Not much time to absorb the finer points of God's call before Paul and Barnabas launched out in response. Well, that's one way to get guidance, but personally, I have reminded the Lord time and again that if he has something for me to do, a complete description of the duties, expectations, and costs of the assignment are the way I prefer to go. To underline my point, I have reminded him of those handy inventions called light bulbs and how they so helpfully illuminate large areas, enabling people to move about without the fear of bumping into unseen dangers. I say, "A brightly lighted call like that would be helpful, Lord. Seeing exactly what's ahead would guarantee my most enthusiastic response." As of this writing, however, it appears that my request is still on back order.

So I am usually left to nose forward in response to small islands of light, just enough, it seems, to allow me to put one foot in front of the other, trusting God to light the next short step when needed. It works pretty well, I will admit, but wouldn't you think God could be made to understand that with a little more light we wouldn't have to bother with so much trust!

Seriously, the question of how and when to respond to partial bits of direction—tiny islands of light—is challenging. When is the right time to launch out and when is it best to wait? Paul, in this passage, may be a good example for us. By the time Acts 13 came around, Paul had heard his call from God in various ways a number of times (Acts 9:15, 16; also note his reflections in 22:17-21 and 26:16-18). Yet, as with many of us, there is often a delay between hearing and comprehending and an additional delay before knowing quite what to do. So having already heard his call, Paul, at the moment of this passage, was ripe for a general nudge from the Holy Spirit to get moving toward it.

Perhaps the message for us is that when God has hinted a calling to us over a period of time, underscoring it through various means, we are poised to respond when he gives the summons, even if his summons, as in this passage, makes only the first few steps clear. This takes courage and a deep degree of trust. Sometimes, after the first step or two forward, our way back to safety has disappeared. Yet responding to these small islands of light, while hard on the heart, is very good for the soul.

Miracles, trust, and a sense of shared adventure with Jesus give life a keen tang. And as we move forward, our way becomes, while perhaps not brighter, at least more sharply focused. In Paul's case, as he proceeded according to his best light, he developed a clearer and clearer sense of his specific calling (Acts 13:44-49; 16:7-10; 18:4-6) and a sharper, cleaner strategy for how to accomplish it. This is the result often testified to by those willing to probe forward into a not yet entirely illuminated call.

KEEP ROWING

Listening to the radio last week, I heard a broadcaster say something helpful. One of the best pieces of advice he ever got, he said, was from his dad, who told him, "Identify your goal, son, and do one thing every day to get there." I like that. Practical. Doable. Determined.

Paul was tenacious in response to his call.

Five times I received from the Jews the forty lashes minus one. Three times I was beaten with rods, once I was stoned, three times I was shipwrecked, I spent a night and a day in the open sea, I have been constantly on the move. I have been in danger from rivers, in danger from bandits, in danger from my own countrymen, in danger from

Gentiles; in danger in the city, in danger in the country, in danger at sea; and in danger from false brothers. I have labored and toiled and have often gone without sleep; I have known hunger and thirst and have often gone without food; I have been cold and naked. Besides everything else, I face daily the pressure of my concern for all the churches (2 Corinthians 11:24-28).

For some of us, a stiff wind is enough to blow us off course. Paul's life calls out, "Don't let obstacles deter you! Don't depart from a chosen direction due to difficulties or vague doubts. Address barriers. Endure them, outlast them."

Paul was not pigheaded about direction. He adjusted course often (Acts 16:7-11; 1 Corinthians 16:3-9). Yet, his adjustments were in response to positive guidance, not deflating discouragements. Paul certainly faced his share of obstacles, but he did not allow them to set his agenda.

Years ago our family went whitewater rafting while on a camping trip in Wyoming. The steersman's instructions have stuck with me regarding the pursuit of my call in Christ. He said, "When the water gets rough—and it is going to get rough— hold on to the oars and keep rowing. This will keep you in the boat and keep the boat moving forward."

That commitment to steady stroking, to doing one thing every day in response to God's leading, will help keep us safely aboard and making consistent headway toward living out our call.

DREAM FOOD, REAL FOOD

In his deeply inspiring autobiography *The Confessions,* Augustine wrote, "Food in our sleep appears like our food awake; yet the sleepers are not nourished by it, for they are asleep."[2]

Sometimes the world around me seems so full of import and consequence. I drive down the road and see more and bigger buildings being erected. I walk through stores and am overwhelmed by the volume of products that lunge at me from the shelves. Everywhere I turn, people are shouting and working hard to make an impression. The TV cries, "Oh! Look at the Internet! The stock market! The Final Four! Hey! What about this movie, the political election, the styles for spring?" The radio shouts, "Listen! Obsess about this hot artist! Get worked up over interest rates, property taxes, the new cars for fall!"

Then I think about God. He is quiet and unassuming. He disappears in the clutter. He does not erect big buildings as shrines to his importance or stun the market with far-out new products. He does not have an agent who gets him lots of airtime. He is not carefully followed in the Nielson ratings or profiled in *The Wall Street Journal.*

The world is bold and brassy, very in your face. God sometimes seems to disappear for days at a time. Sometimes I have actually wondered, *Which is the real world? Where should I place my chips?*

But I have learned to judge things like this: After fifty years in this world, I have tasted lots of what it considers important. A little prestige in work, a nice home, the occasional new car, a few extra dollars, vacations, the rush of getting ahead. Ultimately, as wonderful as they are, these things are like food in dreams. They look great. They even taste good when you eat them. But in the end, they do not satisfy.

Jesus knew that. "Meanwhile his disciples urged him, 'Rabbi, eat something.' But he said to them, 'I have food to eat that you know nothing about.' Then his disciples said to each other, 'Could someone have brought him food?' 'My food,' said Jesus, 'is to do the will of him who sent me and to finish his work'" (John 4:31-34).

Many of us have had a lot of what the world has to offer, yet we are still hungry, restless, dissatisfied, puzzled. We wonder whether, perhaps, the solution is to get bigger helpings of what we have already had. But Jesus reveals an entirely new food. "My food," said Jesus, "is to do the will of him who sent me and to finish his work."

Our food, too, is to do the will of the one who put us here—to love, serve, and reconcile others to God according to our unique call. May we hunger for that food, find it, and be filled.

Lord, you are showing me that there is a song I've been created to sing in your world that no one else knows. There is a bright and lyrical melody you have given me to lift up. You love to help me sing my harmony in the powerful symphony of your creation. Give my song full voice, Lord. Teach my hands and feet and body to play my role. Let my hymn of loving service on earth be the holy and pleasing worship that I will sing to you forever in Heaven.

Amen.

12 SELF-DISCOVERY

One spring day when I was about ten years old, I grabbed a few of my dad's tools and ran to the shore of a nearby lake. There I had been gathering lumber and logs to build a raft to launch in the newly ice-free water.

I got the thing built, and my visions of a leisurely summer idling about on my little craft came to pass. But I remember a distinct feeling of frustration while sawing and pounding that day, a result of not having brought the right tools with me to the lake. Too impatient to go back home, I tried to make do. A stubby, flat-head screwdriver was drafted into service to drive Phillips screws. A hammer with a broken claw allowed me to bend my typical number of nails but not pull them back out again. Frustrating stuff like that.

The memory of clumsiness and aggravation connected with using the wrong tools for the job has always stayed with me. I wonder how many of us experience exasperation and discouragement in life not because there is anything inherently wrong with our activities or careers, but because we are simply the wrong tool for the job?

I once worked for a ministry that held it out as a kind of virtue that those who worked there should disregard their preferences and callings and slot in wherever the ministry was most in need of help. Giftedness and personal call—paying attention to the unique tools in your own tool belt—were only given a passing nod when they happened to coincide with what the ministry demanded at the moment. The result was repeated cases of ineffectiveness, disillusionment, and burnout in good-hearted people.

Each of us is built to do certain things better and with more pleasure and fruitfulness than other things. It is very helpful in discovering our call in Christ to become aware of how we are wired. Passions, gifts, skills, and one's personal way of doing things are important clues to God's calling.

Christians, interestingly, are often nagged by a strange hesitation in this regard. We hear regularly that we should sacrifice personal preferences for the sake of others, forego pleasures, and embrace the cross of Christ, and these all have their place in their proper context. But a misapplication of these ideas can lead us to feel that it is perhaps selfish to pursue work, hobbies, or volunteer activities that we enjoy, feel passionate about, or that come naturally to us. In our desire to be good soldiers, we inadvertently allow self-sacrifice to become more important than God's call. We give ourselves up to the odd notion that struggle, disappointment, and lack of personal fulfillment are somehow more spiritual than personal fruitfulness. I don't know exactly how these ideas get us in their vise grip, but they hold too much sway among us. They tend to paralyze ardent Christians from joyfully searching out and pursuing their calling in Christ.

More and more, however, Christians are understanding that it honors God to live in harmony with how he has created us.

The Bible connects the work God has called us to do with how he has constructed us. "For we are God's workmanship, created in Christ Jesus to do good works, which God prepared in advance for us to do" (Ephesians 2:10).

This, I suppose, should not be startling, yet we often search outside ourselves for special direction when the answer to our call is probably residing quietly within. Becoming aware of our own preferences, strengths, skills, gifts, and personal style is a key piece of identifying our calling in Christ.

This chapter is a little different from those before. Here I've listed a variety of self-discovery questions, each designed to shed some light on a different part of your makeup. These brief activities are by no means exhaustive, but are intended to give you a glimpse into why developing a better self-understanding is central to helping you discern God's call. You are "God's workmanship, created in Christ Jesus to do good works, which God prepared in advance for [you] to do" (Ephesians 2:10).

Let's uncover your tools.

NATURAL STRENGTHS

We begin by pondering your natural strengths and abilities, those that come easily to you, that seem inborn. Think through your response to the following questions, maybe writing down your answers in a notebook.

• What have other people told you that you're good at?

• What projects or activities does it sometimes surprise you to find that other people have a hard time doing?

• Starting in your childhood, what activities or projects have given you pleasure to do?

• What activities or projects are you most apt to volunteer to take on or join in?

• What goals have you achieved? What goals do you find difficult to achieve?

• Drawing from the observations above, create a list of some of your key natural strengths and abilities.

Passions

God often places in us a burden for the people, projects, and needs to which he is calling us. Sometimes this burden or passion is strong and immediate. In other cases, it grows bit by bit, over time. Becoming aware of our inner passions can signal a calling from God.

• What pains in the world do you greatly empathize with? What needs do you become passionate about?

• For what issues and goals would you be willing to endure physical, emotional, or mental suffering?

• Imagine being introduced to a roomful of people. What accomplishments and involvements would you like your introducer to associate with you?

• What work or accomplishments would you like to be remembered for after you die?

• What characters in the Bible speak most loudly and consistently to you? What passions or accomplishments are connected with them?

• Draw from the observations above to create a list of some of your key personal passions.

Spiritual Gifts

A spiritual gift is an ability, talent, or competence through which God especially imparts himself to the church and the world. Spiritual gifts are different from natural strengths and abilities in their particular focus on making God better known and building up the body of Christ. The Bible makes plain that every believer has at least one spiritual gift (I Corinthians 12:4-II, especially v. 7).

Spiritual gifts sometimes correspond to one's natural talents, and sometimes do not. For example, a schoolteacher with a natural talent for teaching might also have the spiritual gift the Bible calls "teaching" (see Romans 12:7), through which God especially empowers the teacher to explain biblical truths with insight and clarity that result in special blessing to the learners. On the other hand, someone with a natural talent for teaching may have a very different spiritual gift for building up the church, maybe giving, helping, healing, wisdom, or others.

On the next page begins a list of spiritual gifts with a reference for where this gift is mentioned in the Bible and a brief description of each. There is no finite list of gifts, and the descriptions vary, so my list and descriptions may be different than some others.

Take time to become familiar with the gifts and descriptions on the chart. Look especially for which gift or gifts best describe you. Then reflect on the questions that follow. They can help you begin to define which spiritual gifts God has given you and which areas of service you operate in most effectively.

✍ A LIST OF SPIRITUAL GIFTS ✍

ADMINISTRATION	I Corinthians 12:28

The ability to bring organization and orderliness to God's work. A talent and passion for guiding details, large and small, toward a desired ministry end.

APOSTLESHIP	Ephesians 4:11

The gift of initiating God's work in new locations. An entrepreneurial ability to plant or extend new works of God where they have not been before.[1]

CREATIVE EXPRESSION	Exodus 31:1-11

An ability to create artistic forms that support and/or express worship to God in public settings.[2]

DISCERNMENT	I Corinthians 12:10

An ability to discern the spirits, distinguishing between good and evil, right and wrong, and the presence or absence of God in statements and intended directions.

ENCOURAGEMENT	Romans 12:8

The gift of building up, encouraging, or inspiring others in their walk with Christ.

EVANGELISM	Ephesians 4:11

An exceptional level of passion and ability to communicate the gospel in a way that leads unbelievers to Christ.

FAITH	I Corinthians 12:9

A distinctive divine enablement to act on God's Word, trusting him to do extraordinary things.

GIVING	Romans 12:8

The desire and ability to give money and/or resources to God's work with exceptional generosity.

HEALING	I Corinthians 12:9

The divine ability to be an agent for physical healing through prayer, touch, or spoken words.

HELPING	I Corinthians 12:28

The gift of functioning in an assisting capacity (often hidden) that supports and meets the needs of others in God's work.

HOSPITALITY	I Peter 4:9, 10

A desire and ability to warmly extend practical expressions of God's love and care (including food, shelter, and interested kindness) to those who enter one's home or ministry setting.

INTERPRETATION OF TONGUES	I Corinthians 12:10

The ability to determine the meaning of a message given to a gathered church body by someone speaking with the gift of tongues (see Tongues).

KNOWLEDGE	I Corinthians 12:8

The ability to sense key, but often hidden, information necessary to counseling or exhorting others in their walk with God.

෴ A LIST OF SPIRITUAL GIFTS ෴

LEADERSHIP	Romans 12:8

The gift of communicating a sense of vision, purpose, direction, and confidence to which others respond in God's work.

MERCY	Romans 12:8

A tendency toward compassion that results in acts of mercy extended to those suffering or in need.

MIRACLES	1 Corinthians 12:10

The ability to trust God with more ease than others to work miracles in needful situations, a result being that the authenticity of God's ministry and message are confirmed.

PROPHECY	Romans 12:6

The ability to speak a uniquely pertinent word of God for direction, repentance, comfort, or encouragement to current or future situations.

SERVICE	Romans 12:7

The tendency to bring a sense of humble, loving helpfulness in one's dealings with others.

PASTORING	Ephesians 4:11

The passion and ability to lovingly guide groups or individuals toward maturity in their walk with God.

TEACHING	Romans 12:7

The ability to explain biblical truths with insight and clarity, resulting in unique spiritual blessing to the learners.

Tongues	1 Corinthians 12:10
The ability to speak a message to a gathered church body in a language especially given by God that is not the language of the listeners. When used in public, this gift is to be exercised in tandem with the gift of interpretation of tongues (1 Corinthians 14:27).	
Wisdom	1 Corinthians 12:8
The ability to apply spiritual truth with insight, discretion, and understanding to groups or individuals.	

In light of the gifts listed on the chart on the previous pages, consider these questions:

• Of the ministry opportunities you have had in the past, which have seemed to bear the most fruitful results?

• Has anybody ever commented that he or she was inwardly blessed through some expression of care or service you rendered to the church or to him or her personally? If so, what service did you provide? In what way was the person blessed? Do you see any of the spiritual gifts described in the list operating here?

• With which of the spiritual gifts described do you most resonate? Which ones make your pulse quicken a little or cause you to respond with an inner *yes*?

GATHER THE RESULTS

With the help of the questions below, review your observations so far:

• What central strengths, abilities, passions, and spiritual gifts emerge?

• Are you aware of any activities God seems to be offering right now where you could test or express these gifts, strengths, and passions? If so, what are they?

• On what level do you sense a calling to these activities? Hobby? Volunteering? Part-time work? Full-time vocation? Other?

⊙ What is one practical, achievable step you will take this week to test and express the strengths, passions, and gifts God has given you?

In addition to questions like these, a variety of classes, surveys, and other tools are available to further help you identify your strengths, passions, gifts, and calling. A few especially good resources include *LifeKeys* by Jane A. G. Kise, David Stark, and Sandra Krebs Hirsh; *Network* by Bruce Bugbee, Don Cousins, and Bill Hybels; and *What You Do Best in the Body of Christ* by Bruce Bugbee. Your church or local Christian bookstore can guide you to these and other helpful resources.

THE MONEY QUESTION

Jim is a product manager for a medical manufacturer in the city where I live. As he was chatting with me in his office one day, his tone became confidential. Leaning close, he said, "I've had it with this job. It is definitely not me." Then he brightened. "But I have a thirteen-year plan. If my profit sharing does well, I will retire from here when I'm fifty-six. Then I'm going to do what I'd really love to do—start an outfitter's store."

Ouch! Jim's comments underscore a pattern I have noticed in many conversations over the years with folks who are pondering new life directions. More often than not, the most challenging issue to living out our calling is not a lack of direction but a reluctance to leave the security of our current source of income.

The question of money has a major impact on our pursuit of calling. Ponder the questions below for any light they might shed on the financial issues surrounding your calling.

• Does the issue of money impact your ability to respond to God's call to exercise your gifts, talents, and passions at this time? If so, how?

• If yours is a question of balancing financial responsibilities while responding to your calling, brainstorm some possible scenarios that would allow you to move forward. (You are not committing to anything at this point!)

• To think more creatively, take yourself out of the situation for a moment. Imagine you are counseling someone else in your position, and all options are open. What are some steps you might suggest to pursue calling while addressing financial barriers?

• If yours is a question of embracing a simpler lifestyle as a trade-off for responding to your calling, reflect on the pros and cons of that choice.

A man approached Jesus one day and thought he would delight the Lord by declaring, "'Teacher, I will follow you wherever you go.' Jesus replied, 'Foxes have holes and birds of the air have nests, but the Son of Man has no place to lay his head'" (Matthew 8:19, 20). Jesus' message? "Friend, count the cost."

There is often a financial consequence to responding to your call. God's idea about calling and money may take you to "God's Money School," a place where students advance through the grades but never entirely graduate! Nothing so exposes our core dependencies as does money.

For those walking out their call, God will time and again use either an abundance or lack of money to encourage us to trade old, broken dependencies for a more authentic trust of him. Along the way, though, doubts and anxieties about money can make war against our call. What do we do? Let me make this suggestion.

There is unusual power in the words of Scripture to unchain our hearts and minds from money hang-ups that loom large and hinder us from living as we are built to live. We often do not need more information or guidance but instead a galvanizing inner power to respond to the call we already hear. The words of the Bible hold this power. They can arouse and embolden something deep inside us that no counselor or any other book can match!

If your sense of call endures after counsel and prayer (and is consistent with your gifts, strengths, and passions), yet financial issues seem to make responding impractical, spend regular periods prayerfully reflecting on passages like the ones below. They help people like you and me, facing situations way beyond our strength, to find ways to move forward with God. Using the Bible reflection methods described in chapters 4 and 5, reflect on Genesis 17:1-22; Joshua 1:1-9; Judges 7:1-22; Matthew 7:7-11; Luke 12:16-34; Hebrews 11. These are just a few of the many passages in Scripture that can rouse courage to trust God for all we need as we obey his call.

Money alone must never be allowed to stand in the way of calling. Gain strength and courage to probe ahead, a step at a time, trusting God to support your path. Boldly ask God to create a way forward. A wonderful experience of his power and care await you!

Dear Jesus, what an unexpected honor it is that you call us to be allies in your work! You made the universe without need for anyone's help, yet you are not satisfied until we work alongside you. You sustain the world in every way from moment to moment, yet crave us to be partners in its nourishment. Lord, grow in me the strengths, passions, and gifts that let me take my place in the living and serving body that works beside you to feed your life to a famished world.

Amen.

SATISFIED

He has filled the hungry with good things.
Luke 1:53

13 TRANSFORMATION

Screeeeeech! Crunch! These days the sound of squealing tires and crunching metal makes me cringe. But as a sixteen-year-old passenger in the back seat of another fellow's car, I thought it was kind of exciting.

On a springtime Sunday afternoon, some high school friends and I were being driven to a conference in another city by a youth worker, an adult named John. A few moments earlier, as we floated along a Minnesota state highway in his new silver-gray Buick LeSabre, John had been bubbling with enthusiasm for the spiritual conference we were about to attend. Suddenly a car pulled out from a side road just ahead. John could neither stop nor avoid it, and a split second later we smashed into its rear bumper.

After the stunned silence that often follows a collision, John turned to make sure we were all OK. Then he bolted from the car in the direction of the other driver, a young woman with a couple of kids in the back seat. It was at this moment that I got my very first eyewitness view of spiritual transformation—though maybe not of the sort I want to encourage in this chapter. Where a moment before John was a picture of Christian love and good humor, he was now transformed into a roaring, offended driver. He unholstered his prosecuting skills (unfortunately for the young woman, between Sundays John was an attorney) and blasted her with threats of legal action.

As young observers, we were stunned. For my part, I couldn't reconcile the furious scene in front of me with the lovefest we had all been enjoying in the car a few moments before. I must admit, I found myself wondering who our friend John really was, and whether Christian love did not after all apply in the case of car crashes.

I understand now, from a distance of many years, that John's faith, while real, had simply not yet sent its roots very deeply into his life. While God's love in John included giving up a Sunday afternoon to take some rowdy teenagers a few miles to a church event, it apparently did not yet extend to showing mercy to someone who had just bent the left front fender of his new car.

For the rest of the day, John was withdrawn, distracted, and touchy. I can only guess he was wrestling with a residue of anger from the accident. Or perhaps the incongruity between his faith convictions and his reaction to the fender bender was galling and embarrassing, causing him to turn inward. At any rate, a battle between opposing forces was evident within him, and on that particular day there seemed no clear winner.

So, who was John? Was he a loving guy reaching out selflessly to a group of searching teenagers on God's behalf? Or was he an irate prosecutor, ready to drag a terrified young woman over the legal coals? The answer, of course, is that John was both. He was a fallen human being in whom the Spirit of God had been born and was beginning a program of inner transformation. He was something old existing alongside something new. He was Dr. Jekyll and Mr. Hyde. He was like me. Maybe he was also like you.

A NEW COUNTRY

An important part of our life in Christ is the hopeful expectation of a changed life. The Bible tells us that as human beings, we have the imprint of eternity upon our hearts (Ecclesiastes 3:11). This heavenly imprint constantly whispers into our souls a vision of life as it is intended to be. Though we often feel fragmented and incomplete, we sense that somewhere there exists a life of wholeness. We are often worn out inside by passions that clash with one another, goals that conflict, and desires that race in opposite directions. Yet, our heavenly intuition tells us of a place of focus, convergence, and rest.

For those who ask Christ to remake their lives, this passion for life in the new country seems to intensify. We increasingly long for a transformation of our attitudes, values, and desires. We hope for the healing of pains and wounds that cause us inner suffering. We ask God to remodel us within so the reality of our daily experience may be more in harmony with our identity as his sons and daughters.

Jesus affirms this longing for completeness. He said, "Be perfect, therefore, as your heavenly Father is perfect" (Matthew 5:48). Wow! There's an expectation for you! Yet, doesn't Jesus' admonition simply correspond with our own deep desire for the wholeness and holiness we have begun to taste in him? Isn't Jesus underscoring our consistent longing for spiritual, mental, and emotional transformation?

Still, how do we get from here to there? How do we move from a life often marked by hyper self-concern, that spins out all sorts of behaviors hurtful to ourselves and others, toward a life that breathes the wholeness and love offered in Jesus? Further, how do we find healing for the wounds and pains out of which our sinful behaviors arise? The Bible seems to affirm that such a new way of living is possible.

Paul says, "Therefore, if anyone is in Christ, he is a new creation; the old has gone, the new has come!" (2 Corinthians 5:17). But sometimes I don't feel so new. Sometimes I'm glad people can't look inside and see the old me still rattling around. What is the path from my old self to my new self in Christ? How do I exchange the ruinous loves, habits, addictions, and coping devices that lock me into destructive patterns of living for the complete life ("complete" is perhaps a more accurate translation of Jesus' word *perfect* quoted above) that is mine as a child of God?

Well, one approach to transformation, enduringly popular with Christians throughout the centuries, is to go on the warpath. To identify our many sins and failures, imperfections and pains, and devote ourselves to rooting them out.

In the novel *Godric,* Frederick Buechner gives us a glimpse of this method of attempted self-transformation. In the course of his travels, Godric, the novel's main character, meets the hermit Elric. Over the years, Elric has become fixated on his own sinfulness and the constant temptations to his soul. Elric devotes every moment of every day to a relentless war against his demons, prodded by a sense of obligation to make himself perfect before God. On his deathbed, a realization of his misplaced focus dawns on Elric and results in a sorry admission: "May God have mercy on my soul. I fear in Paradise I'll even miss the fiends!"[1] Elric's fixation on his own sinfulness turned his demons into idols.

A longing for inner liberation, together with a sense of responsibility to become "perfect as he is perfect," can have an Elric effect on our lives. Rather than developing a growing taste for Jesus Christ, we instead simply develop a nose for sin and self-failure. Intent on inner change, we exchange a love affair with God for a program of religious self-improvement. We probably make some progress toward better behavior, better thinking, even better serving of others, but it is a rather lonely climb up a very steep hill. We become more "correct" but less happy, more "perfect" but much less alive in the joy of a gracious relationship with God. Is there a better way?

THE UPWARD GAZE

It has been said, "Let us glance at sin, but gaze at Christ." This sentiment, I think, begins to move us along the path toward inner transformation. When we hurt terribly inside from the wounds of life, when we are embarrassed by the clinging effects of sin, and when we are made tired by our seeming lack of progress with God, a natural response may be to focus on our state within. It is at this moment that we must (sometimes, by sheer force of will) tear our eyes away from our unfortunate inner state and begin to fix them on Jesus himself. Power for change, a willingness to release old coping devices, and the inspiration to embrace the cross of Christ in the way our ills require are made possible by a personal, growing vision of Jesus Christ.

Awhile ago, on the radio, I heard the true story of Anne and her husband, Tom. Anne and Tom had been married for about ten years when one day, at the grocery store, Anne bumped into an old boyfriend, Mark. As they stood by the frozen yogurt case, Anne noticed a tiny thrill in her heart. They chatted for a few minutes and then said an awkward good-bye.

The next day, while Anne's husband was at work, the phone rang. It was Mark. In spite of an insistent inner warning *ping*, Anne spent forty-five minutes pouring out her life to Mark and listening as Mark did the same. Soon they were trading calls nearly every day, and in a little while meeting for lunch two or three times a week. Before long Anne found she could think of nothing but her old boyfriend. She loved her husband, but her attraction to Mark had become overwhelming.

Anne told herself she mustn't think of him—it had to stop; she wouldn't see him anymore. But the pull of this dangerous relationship was too strong. Now all the warning flags were flying. Before it became too late, Anne decided she had to talk with her husband about Mark. That night, at the kitchen table, Anne laid everything before Tom.

"I can't stop thinking about him, Tom," Anne said. "I'm afraid. He excites me so much."

Tom was quiet for a long time. Then he took his wife's hands in his own and said, very softly, "I'm so sorry, Anne. I'm sorry I can't do that for you anymore."

Anne looked at her husband in shock. This was not the response she had been bracing for. Suddenly Anne glimpsed a fresh vision of the treasure she had in her own husband. She rose that very moment, called Mark on the phone, and told him in her husband's presence, "Never call me again. I will never speak with you again."

Someone wisely once said that sin is not overcome by discipline but by inspiration. Good intentions, stern vows, and even accusing self-guilt could not produce in Anne what a new love for her husband accomplished in a single moment. As her eyes were newly opened for her husband, the attractive power of her competing lover dissolved away.

This is also true in our relationship with Christ. If we hope to have any chance against the many substitute loves that compete to lure us from the husband of our souls, we must somehow replace the attraction of these lesser loves with a greater love. We need to realize that guilt, fear, duty, self-discipline, and similar motivators are not powerful or consistent enough to counteract the hurts, temptations, and natural self-love that work to divorce our hearts from Christ. Only a growing inner vision of Jesus himself can do that. "Let us fix our eyes on Jesus, the author and perfecter of our faith, who for the joy set before him endured the cross, scorning its shame, and sat down at the right hand of the throne of God. Consider him who endured such opposition from sinful men, so that you will not grow weary and lose heart" (Hebrews 12:2, 3).

There is a sense relayed in the Bible that as we develop an inward gaze on Jesus Christ, give our attention to him, relax in his presence, and rejoice in his company, we will increasingly resemble the one upon whom we focus. "And we, who with unveiled faces all reflect the Lord's glory, are being transformed into his likeness with ever-increasing glory, which comes from the Lord, who is the Spirit" (2 Corinthians 3:18).

The intimacy that leads to inner transformation is given a picture by Jesus in the Gospel of John. In John 15:5 Jesus says, "I am the vine; you are the branches. If a man remains in me and I in him, he will bear much fruit."

Picture the living, potent, organic connection between a vine and its branches. Imagine the sap that flows from the vine, carrying nourishment and ultimately producing fruit in the branch. What does the branch do to grow the fruit? The vine's answer is simple: "Remain in me." Stay put. Cling to the vine. Relax. And drink deeply. Lasting inner change results over time from a restful, connected relationship with Jesus Christ.

An Enlarged Home

Still, is there nothing the Christian should do to be an active partner with God in the work of inner transformation? Are we to simply love God and assume he'll change what he wants, when he wants? Is inner transformation automatic?

Well, yes. And no. While inner change flows naturally from my relationship with God, in this process of change I do have a vigorous *responsive* role to play. In the remaining chapters, we will consider a variety of cooperative inner postures that allow God room to work transformation in our lives. They include surrender, rest, embracing God in suffering, responsiveness to his guidance, and more.

As we move toward these topics, let me make a few early comments about one posture that seasons the others and is at the very heart of inner transformation—developing a habit of responsiveness to God's Spirit. "If anyone loves me, he will obey my teaching. My Father will love him, and we will come to him and make our home with him" (John 14:23).

From time to time in our relationship with God, a sense of calling arises, a feeling of conviction about a new way the Spirit is inviting us to live. These are precious moments. If we respond positively to these overtures, we find that God, in a certain sense, enlarges his home inside us. We find we are supplied with spiritual, emotional, and practical resources to help us walk forward into a transformed experience of life. Gripping fears diminish; self-concerns lessen. Old pains and inner wounds become salved by his company. A growing trustfulness and confidence in the reality and sufficiency of God begins to firm up inside.

Yet, here is a key—we must be content to listen with patient attention to God and act only *in response* to his guidance. Actions taken in response to God are surrounded, uplifted, and made possible by his grace. On the other hand, if we arbitrarily construct our own religious rules about how to live, we set up a legal system of dos and don'ts, rights and wrongs, which he has not empowered us to live. The result is much spiritual heavy lifting with little to show for the effort. Inner transformation, on the other hand, flows from the grace that cycles through our lives as we interact responsively with God. In a later chapter we will spend time with Moses, observing the gradual transformation available to those who learn, like him, to live responsively with the Spirit.

A DEEPER TRANSFORMATION

There are times, though, when transformation simply doesn't come, times when our hunger for a new way to be remains unfed. At these times, we certainly feel called to a new way of life and are desirous for change. We earnestly try to listen and cooperate with God. We do this, we do that, but we're still the same inside. We still hurt; we still fall and still feel far from the mark. We work the problem from a thousand different angles, but our lack of inner change is bewildering. We guess that perhaps we haven't tried hard enough or that we've missed understanding some special insight that would set us free. A tendency, during such times, is to hike up our resolve and throw ourselves over and over again at our problem. Yet, after penetrating it a little, we bounce back like a rubber ball to the place we started, where we scratch our heads in confused discouragement.

For those times, let me suggest a different approach. It is this: simply rest with God in your problem. Simply be with him in your sin, your emptiness, your failure. Rest quietly with him in your confusion, your paralysis. Sit next to him in the wound that won't heal, the pain that won't subside, the desert that never ends.

This is transformation of another sort, of a deeper kind. Here the still center of your love affair with Jesus Christ rests steady, unmoved, unquenched, unconquered by your unresolved messes. Here your love for God really does take precedence. It is no longer a means to an end, a kind of convenient tool to work your own liberation. Here, instead, as the apostle Paul says, "I consider everything a loss compared to the surpassing greatness of knowing Christ Jesus my Lord, for whose sake I have lost all things. I consider them rubbish, that I may gain Christ" (Philippians 3:8).

Sometimes, our very desire to be transformed into the new creation God wants us to be must be considered rubbish in comparison with simply knowing Christ. Is it enough for you to simply love him? To draw close to him, to offer him your affection? If intimately abiding with Jesus produced no change at all within you, could you be satisfied to simply remain with him in your painful, unresolved stuff?

The Bible says that the Holy Spirit is given to believers as a promise of things to come. The appetite for eternity that the Spirit stirs inside us is both fed and increased by the measured tastes of transformation we experience in this lifetime. And whatever transformation we enjoy will be the reflection of God's face upon our features as we continually cast a loving eye upward. "And we, who with unveiled faces all reflect the Lord's glory, are being transformed into his likeness with ever-increasing glory, which comes from the Lord, who is the Spirit" (2 Corinthians 3:18).

The increasing gaze of our lives upon Jesus Christ—patient, loving, sacrificial, and constant—draws us resolutely toward eternity, where the Spirit's promise of our ultimate transformation will one day be fully realized: "Dear friends, now we are children of God, and what we will be has not yet been made known. But we know that when he appears, we shall be like him, for we shall see him as he is" (1 John 3:2).

Dear Jesus, who I am is not who I was. And where I'm going is not where I was once headed. I am someone new on my way to a transformed place. Yes, I dare say that. And tomorrow I'll be newer yet. Lord, I look in amazement at the things that were once so attractive to me. Where did it go, the importance they seemed to have? How did it fly away, the fascination they once held? There is no answer, Lord, but you. You, who speak love while calling me forth! You, who sing over me for joy as I become slowly more real. You, who have quickened my heart by the warmth of your breath and the glance of your eyes. To your arms, Jesus, I have come and have found my home.

Amen.

14 SURRENDER

It's told that Victor Hugo, the great French novelist of the nineteenth century, was sitting in his study one sunny morning when he heard a tap-tap-tapping against the window. Rising to investigate, he discovered a lone bee, trapped inside, flinging himself repeatedly against the glass in an attempt to get to the garden beyond. On the floor beneath the window lay a half-dozen dead bees that had pursued a similar strategy before running out of gas.

Hugo lifted a napkin from a table and attempted to capture the bee to guide it out an open window. The bee frantically plunged this way and that in an attempt to escape. Eventually Hugo was able to gently grasp the frightened bee and slip him through the window. In a moment, the bee was floating freely about the garden.

Gazing at the freed prisoner, Hugo reflected on the similarities between his relationship with the bee and God's relationship with human beings. The bee, trapped in a predicament beyond his understanding, longed to be free. To that end, he was working all the angles he could. Hugo, from his broader perspective, could see that the bee had no chance for freedom pursuing his present path. Yet, when Hugo tried to help, the bee wouldn't have it. He went into crazy gyrations and would have stung the hand trying to help him if he could. The bee's irrational fear would have doomed him to join his dead friends on the floor if Hugo had not persisted in his role as underappreciated bee savior.

What should an enlightened bee have done? How might he have gained his freedom and saved himself the bumps and bruises he later sat nursing in his beehive? An enlightened bee would have realized his dilemma and the uselessness of his own solutions and would have submitted to the nice man with the napkin trying to help out. Yet that would have meant a risk. It would have meant surrendering himself into the hands of the strange creature towering over him—a creature with the power to liberate him or squash him out of existence. Given the options, an unenlightened bee chose to fight.

It is a little mortifying to have so much in common with a honeybee. Time and again, in the middle of my predicaments, I find myself fighting the nice man with the napkin. It is a battle I can't win, of course. If I seem to win, I really lose. If I buzz and sting until he withdraws, I have only set myself up to join my dead friends on the floor. It has taken me a long time to understand that there are certain battles for which the road to victory is the way of surrender.

Surrender. The word has about it something of the sense of adversaries and battle. And while in the chapters of this book we do not usually think of our relationship with God in such terms, I would suggest that we now turn our attention to those moments in our lives when we find ourselves struggling in opposition to God. Resistant, independent, contrary. Beating our wings against the glass. Those are the bitter moments of a relationship with God. And our sour behavior in them tends to keep us from God's table, isolated and unfed. Since episodes like this so often find their way into our experience, we are probably due to give them some time.

The ultimate destination of spiritual surrender is liberty—rescue, emancipation, and freedom. Down the path of surrender wait surprising solutions for the journey of life. But along the way, surrender to God takes us temporarily through some territory that can make our flesh cringe. This is because surrendering ourselves to God involves touching the cross of Christ to our stubborn, anxious, and sometimes delicate places. Jesus told his disciples, "If anyone would come after me, he must deny himself and take up his cross and follow me. For whoever wants to save his life will lose it, but whoever loses his life for me will find it" (Matthew 16:24, 25).

Surrender is the great separator. It is the doorway through which sleepy religious curiosity becomes wide-awake personal commitment. It is the master key that fits each door in the castle, allowing the king to enter every room. Spiritual surrender is to God what the patient's consent is to the doctor—it allows him to sharpen his tools and start the operation.

DEFYING SURRENDER

The old movie comedian W. C. Fields was on his deathbed when a friend came to visit one day. Fields was not known to be a religious man, so the friend was surprised to find him reading a Bible. "Fields!" exclaimed the man, "What are you doing with that Bible?" To which Fields replied, "Looking for loopholes."

Many of us would breathe easier if we could discover a loophole or two in God's insistence that we surrender our lives so entirely into his hands. About three or four years into my own pursuit of God, I came across *The Cross and Sanctification*[1] by the late T. A. Hegre, co-founder of a longtime missions organization based in Minneapolis. This book was Hegre's argument that Christians do not have the option to pick and choose which of God's commands we want to obey, but that God's will must become our will in all the large and small decisions of life. No exceptions. No apologies. Next topic, please.

At that time I had the strong impression that God was urging me to obey him in several specific areas of my life, a couple that were relatively minor and one quite serious. To follow his lead, I felt, would probably mean a variety of unpleasant consequences. These I was anxious to avoid if at all possible.

But reading Hegre's book, I found no escape. He quoted this Bible verse and that, and made this argument and the next, each aimed, it seemed, directly at me and my struggle of wills with God. When it became apparent about halfway through the book that Hegre was going to be narrow-minded and not allow a special exception in my case, I began to argue with him. For example, Hegre quoted (to my intense irritation) verses like this from Paul: "I have been crucified with Christ and I no longer live, but Christ lives in me. The life I live in the body, I live by faith in the Son of God, who loved me and gave himself for me" (Galatians 2:20).

Hegre maintained that verses like this indicate that as Christians we are called to adopt a way of life in which our own often self-serving desires should be consistently crucified in preference to God's. At first glance, I had to admit that biblically Hegre seemed to hold the high ground. But I was young and up to the challenge. Barely breaking a sweat, for every scriptural precedent Hegre called on, I would counter, "Of course, my friend, of course. But you know, a broad-minded person could look at that passage another way too." Then I would proceed to find an interpretation that served my secret desire not to submit to God on the point at issue.

Finally, about two-thirds of the way through Hegre's book, it occurred to me that I was imitating W. C. Fields. While, on the one hand, I was being pulled toward a malleable, responsive, surrendered relationship with God, on the other I was looking for loopholes, trying to discredit God's call for a surrendered lifestyle in order to free myself to live as I preferred.

I've noticed that I'm not the only person to have fought this battle with God. Most Christians would attest to some version of it. In fact, recorded history is the repeated narrative of humankind's struggle of wills with God. The question of who is going to be God, of who will submit to whom, is one of the two or three most important issues to be settled in the lives of those desiring an intimate experience of God.

As I mentioned, of specific concern to me as I read Hegre's book were several issues over which I was especially engaged in a tug-of-war with God. There were undoubtedly a hundred other areas of my life in which I was also out of step with God, but these several represented my prevailing determination to run my life the way I wanted. If God could help me surrender these specific issues to him, it would represent a general widening of permission for him to take up the reigns of my entire life.

One area of struggle had to do with my relationship with Gerri, who was my fiancée at that time. For some reason, I was haunted by the idea that I might somehow lose her. It's hard to say exactly how this fear gripped me, but I couldn't shake it. I feared Gerri might lose interest in me, or might die, or in some other way be capriciously taken away from me by God. I often found myself pleading, "God—above all things, don't let me lose Gerri!" I felt obsessively protective but also helpless at what God might deal me in regard to her.

God was very plain with me. He let me know that I needed to release my future with Gerri into his hands, giving him permission to do with her as he pleased. I understand now that God was able to look ahead and see my tendency as an insecure human to pervert love into control in an attempt to get my needs met. Knowing I had my hand on the handle of something dangerous, God said, "C'mon, Joel—yield it to me. You've got to release your relationship with Gerri. I'll take care of it, you know."

But this seemed risky. Although I knew I couldn't control

her love for me or our future together, still, I felt if I gave God permission to do with her what he would, well, who knew what he might pull?

This is fairly representative of the inner battles we find ourselves waging with God. The issues we need to surrender often don't involve gross sin. Typically they simply have to do with some area in which God offers himself in exchange for a coping device we've been relying on to get our needs met. When we're in the middle of negotiating this exchange, it can feel terribly risky. We've become best friends with our coping devices, our God-substitutes. They seem to be the only way we can get through life. The idea of giving them up makes us feel defenseless, naked to the world. Don't shoot me—I'm just the messenger—but I am sorry to have to report that if we walk with God long enough, such exchanges will be required in every area of our lives.

Ultimately, surrender to God always results in a broad new way of living. At the moment of choosing, however, God seems to offer no firm guarantees about how things will work out. Bible teacher Bob Mumford pictures surrendering to God as the signing of a contract. God hands us a contract, giving him permission to take charge of our lives. We look it over and immediately notice something odd. It's blank—no terms, no conditions, no writing at all. Only a place to sign. We say, "Um, pardon me, Lord, I don't mean to embarrass you, but you seem to have made a mistake. This contract is blank." To which God replies, "That's right. You sign now; I'll fill in the terms later."

Uh-oh!

In seeking our signature, God is posing one of the most important questions of our lives. "Child," says the Lord, "you've tried for a long time without success to run your own life, but now I ask you—in the future, which of us is going to be God? By this I mean, who will be allowed to set the agenda? Which one will be served? Whose wishes will be honored? Who will have the final say-so? Which of us will be God?"

God knows that how you come down on this question will have a more dramatic effect on the rest of your life than perhaps any other single decision you'll make as a Christian. Later there will be questions regarding what it means to obey God in given situations, and you will be called to reaffirm your surrender many times, in many ways. You also will face the challenge of discerning God's voice from the many others that will call for your obedience (society, family, obstructive spirits, even the church).

But the first question is "Will I give God the right, regardless of personal consequences, to be in control of my life?"

I have noticed that Christians often criticize other faiths that don't require their members to be accountable to the absolute, biblical authority of God. But the fact is that most Christians, regardless of their orthodoxy, have also found ways to remain their own gods. They have found ways to bob and weave safely around inconvenient commands, slip past hard sayings, and stay a step or two ahead of the rough weight of the cross. Yet this is deadly to a relationship with God. It's like allowing a child to tell the doctor how much treatment he'll accept, or letting a soldier dictate to a commander in what capacity he'll serve. It is an inversion of the relationship. It results in an up-and-down, inconsistent, frustrating experience.

So God's first question is "Who's in charge here?"

As I struggled against this question in my battle with Hegre's book, I eventually admitted to myself that I was looking for loopholes, trying to get around the fact that God had the ultimate right to ask of me anything he wanted. That admission marked a new beginning for me. Somehow, from that point forward, I decided not to defend myself from the truth any longer. I decided to accept whatever appeared, on objective consideration, to be God's guidance for me—regardless of the personal consequences.

This decision seemed supported by this passage that I discovered at just that time: "Do you not know that your body is a temple of the Holy Spirit, who is in you, whom you have received from God? You are not your own; you were bought at a price" (1 Corinthians 6:19, 20).

"You are not your own; you were bought at a price." While before such sentiments would have sent me fleeing for the hills, they now somehow focused and distilled for me what it meant to be a human being in relationship with God. If I still reserved the right to seal off selected areas of my life from God's authority, that privilege melted with the embrace of this passage.

LIVING SURRENDER

I began now, as well as I knew how, to respond to God in those areas in which I had been resisting him. I gave God permission, for example, to do in my relationship with Gerri whatever he saw fit. I stepped trembling into that moment of surrender when, by a choice of will, you open your hands, releasing the thing you have been strenuously protecting, with no guarantee you'll ever get it back. When I did so, that remarkable relief that always results from no longer playing God entered my soul. I found that I did not love Gerri any less but more genuinely, and could begin to delight in our relationship as a gift to be received rather than a possession to be guarded.

In other areas, as I yielded to God's counsel, a few of the unpleasant consequences that I had dreaded did occur—painful, embarrassing, but not fatal. And I began to find a consistent closeness and progress in my relationship with God that had not been there before. It felt good to leave the doors and windows of my heart unbolted to his visits—whatever those visits might bring. And as I became increasingly home to him, I noticed that he was at home, too, when I went to call. Over time a sort of camaraderie began to develop between us, the closeness felt between two friends who share a dangerous adventure. These and other benefits of obedient surrender we will discuss further in following chapters.

But I experienced one thing in particular that is important to share at this point. I found that God was on my side. I found he was kind and did not take advantage of me in my new willingness to obey him. Some of us feel that if we give God permission to ask of us what he will—who knows what he might ask us to do! Who knows where he might send us, how he might want to use us, what he might demand of us, and so on. We've generated our own personal horror lists about what God might have in mind for us. These fears usually aren't connected with anything he really intends. Instead they are born out of our own insecurities, but while we are struggling with them, that is not so easy to see. All we can see are the ominous possibilities that connect God's will for us with the most distasteful, embarrassing, unrewarding scenarios we can imagine.

But is this how Jesus treated people in the Gospels? Is this the testimony of Christians who unreservedly follow him today? Contrary to what certain voices would like you to believe, God is on your side. He built you. He understands you. He deeply empathizes with your needs. It is true that he won't protect you from everything that you may wish to be protected from. It is also true that he will frequently ask you to leave the safety of your fireside. Yet, even as your hands accept the irons that result in your inner crucifixion, God envelops you in his care. This is the great paradox of surrender: our cross is the total abandonment that leads to our deep embrace, the killing that becomes our consolation, and the destruction of our flesh (Romans 7:18) that sets our spirits free. I have yet to meet a person who has surrendered himself to Jesus' cross who has regretted that decision.

In the novel *The Voyage of the Dawn Treader*, part of "The Chronicles of Narnia," C. S. Lewis tells the story of a naughty boy named Eustace. This young fellow has been so bad for so long and has rejected the advice of the lion Aslan (the God-figure in the book) so many times that one morning he wakes up to find he has outwardly become the thing he inwardly resembles—a selfish, deceitful dragon.

Well, now, Eustace doesn't know what to do. His friends don't recognize him, so they flee. A bracelet he had stolen and was wearing at the time of his transformation is now much too small on his large dragon arm and pains him terribly. He has nowhere to turn until finally, in the presence of Aslan, Eustace repents of his former behavior.

Aslan bares a long, sharp claw and plunges it deep into Eustace's dragon body. The great lion then proceeds to tear away the skin, painfully liberating the boy from his scaly prison. Eustace said later that the claw that freed him hurt terribly—and felt wonderful too.

I've felt that claw. Everyone who habitually surrenders to God will feel that claw free them from the thousand phantoms and fears that clamor for us to manipulate, coerce, and hide our way through life. Sometimes it doesn't hurt to be set free. Sometimes it does. But it is always a great relief. Those who experience that freedom do not want to go back.

Lord, this tight, labored grip I use to protect my precious self-rule has worn me out. But what would my life be without my independence? How would I get by without my little sin, my all-important addiction, my soothing obsessions? You used to look past them but now you are stern. Your eyes tell me it's time to choose between them and you. Lord, I can only speak a very small yes. Still, what I can do I will. I choose to give you permission, now, to erect your cross inside me, to touch my heart with that rough, reviving wood. Give me courage to taste the death that lets me rise from this tomb of lifeless dependencies into the freedom of those who surrender themselves—heart, soul, mind, and strength—fully, Lord, to you.

Amen.

15 SUFFERING

Ellie's gnarled fingers traced a faint, repeating pattern on the arm of her wheelchair. In her dim nursing home room, my new friend, frail and fading, spoke of a life gone by. Eventually the subject turned to her fragile health and likely soon death.

"Oh, I'm ready," she said with some weariness. "I've had enough!"

Talking further, it became clear that Ellie was not referring to just her physical suffering, but to the whole long, weary problem of living. More than ninety years of dilemmas, predicaments, and disagreeable surprises had just about used up her good humor. Death no longer seemed something to avoid but a final, melancholy release from a lengthy, exhausting chore. Ellie had come to the firm conviction that the threescore and ten we are allowed for our sojourn through this world is plenty, given the nature of the place. She was ready to call it a day.

Would it be too extreme to say that this life is one long suffering? We hurt. Life hurts. The blows life delivers inflict pain on us on every level. Our more visible, physical sufferings are outstripped by our sufferings within. It hurts to feel uncertain. It hurts to deeply care. It hurts to peer ahead and anguish in doubt. Rejections, refusals, withdrawals, people we love in pain creating a second helpless pain in us.

Ours is a world gone seriously haywire. Humankind's rejection of God, as described in the early chapters of Genesis, has resulted in an experience on this earth that in many ways expresses the personality of the one—Satan—with whom we have chosen to dance: confusion; frustration; jealous cruelty; fumbled chances; staggering, random, and seemingly pointless suffering. Most of us, caught up like civilians in a war we didn't sign up for, are just looking for a safe place to hide.

Making the problem worse is the question of why God doesn't do anything about it.

I looked and saw all the oppression that was taking place under the sun:

I saw the tears of the oppressed—
    and they have no comforter;
power was on the side of their oppressors—
    and they have no comforter.
And I declared that the dead,
    who had already died,
are happier than the living,
    who are still alive.
But better than both
    is he who has not yet been,
who has not seen the evil
    that is done under the sun.

                —Ecclesiastes 4:1-3

Some have a hard time escaping the feeling that God is behind their suffering, nearly enjoying the show. "The arrows of the Almighty are in me, my spirit drinks in their poison; God's terrors are marshaled against me" (Job 6:4).

Throughout this book, we have made the point time and again that God can be trusted because he is good. He is on our side, zealous for our interests. Most of us want to believe that. Intuitively we sense that in God's powerful goodness lies our safety, our fulfillment. Yet, sometimes we can't help wondering. Just look in the newspapers or at TV. The pain seems overwhelming, paralyzing. Look at my family. Look at my own life.

Though we want God to be good, the evidence might make it a close case in court. To add to our frustration, he seems so unconcerned. He does not put forward explanations for the problem of suffering that fully absolve him or entirely satisfy us. We are pretty much left to accept life as it is, trusting ourselves to his love, seeming contradictions and all.

Personally, I have butted my head against the problem of pain for thirty years, trying to uncover an explanation both rationally and emotionally satisfying—an explanation that harmonizes the fact of suffering with the truth of a powerful God who loves me. Though I come up with ideas that work on paper—humankind's free will has launched us on this forewarned journey with all its tragic consequences—a pat theology of suffering doesn't soothe the raw angst I feel so often as a citizen of this distressed globe.

It has slowly dawned on me over the years that the very fact that God himself puts so little energy into constructing soothing, rational defenses for the existence of suffering is, perhaps, an important clue to understanding the subject. I don't mean that God avoids the topic. Hardly. The Bible is thick with it. But God's counsel there regarding suffering—*explanation* is perhaps not the best word due to its focus on intellectual understanding— is always in connection with something bigger.

Suffering, in the Bible, never stands alone as a self-contained experience. It is not a swatch of pain to be avoided or endured, but a binding thread in a complex fabric. It is not a bitter dish to be traded, if possible, in favor of something sweeter, but a tart ingredient required by a greater recipe. God desires us to live in broader lands, to swim deeper seas. Suffering, in the Bible, is one gift among many that God uses to lure us out of our small caves of self-focus into the expansive landscape he calls Redemption. Because the impact of suffering on our lives will be either hugely positive or hugely negative, depending upon our response to it, God's counsel in the Bible tends to be concerned with our inner posture toward this often unwelcome table guest.

Ultimately, suffering is about relationship. In fact, like love, suffering is impossible to understand *apart* from relationship. When love is poked and prodded, analyzed and dissected, it does not reveal its magic. But when love is lived out in relationship, it becomes something organic that grows intimacy between the lovers. The same is true of suffering. God's counsel to sufferers is not tailored to expand your mind but your relationship with him.

A disclaimer: Those demanding to think the problem of suffering to its knees before allowing it to teach their hearts will very likely find a better discussion of the subject somewhere else. (If you are the first to find the Big Answer, by the way, I will gladly put all calls on hold to take yours!) For those willing, on the other hand, to live the problem of suffering, to embrace it, to let it knead and massage their souls toward a more intimate experience of God and others, this chapter might hold some small pieces of help.

Jesus is our key point of reference for living our suffering. Jesus' sufferings during his years of ministry on earth, and particularly during his final hours, hold many open doorways through which we may pass into a more satisfying, redemptive experience of our trials and afflictions. In this chapter, we will walk alongside Jesus as he struggles under, accepts, and is transformed by his own suffering, becoming the elder brother who shows the way to his younger siblings.

SHARED SUFFERING

For many months before the eighteen or so hours of his intense final suffering, Jesus meditated on what lay ahead (Matthew 16:21; Mark 9:31). We are not admitted very deeply into those personal moments between Jesus and his Father, but the Bible shows that their fellowship was rich and frequent (Matthew 14:23; Mark 1:35; Luke 6:12). This points to the first lesson that Jesus teaches us about suffering: afflictions are never to be endured alone. They are to be experienced under the care of a loving Father.

For ten years, Don worked as a missionary in a remote East Asian country. One day, home on furlough, sitting in a parked car in a closed garage, Don turned the key and waited for the fumes to take his life. What a mystery! I tread this story lightly, not allowed to know all that passed between Don and the Lord before his death. What those who were close to him suspect is that Don had gradually become overwhelmed by the needs of the people with whom he worked and his inability to make the impact he thought he should. More and more, Don believed he had failed God. The unmet needs of the people he served and his perceived failure caused Don intense inner suffering. In the end, the massive weight of his isolated pain was more than he could endure.

Many of us have inherited a religious, social, and even gender culture that urges us to bear our suffering silently, like good soldiers. Our heroes are those who suffer stoically, as though proof of their deep spirituality. This leads to a tendency to "perform" our suffering for God rather than invite him into it. But our griefs must not be privately endured, rather *shared* in communion with our Father and others. Ultimately, it was not Don's pain that led to his death, but his aloneness in it— the paralyzing sense of no aid, no comfort, and especially no Comforter.

We will always seek, in one way or another, to escape suffering we believe we must bear alone. Jesus teaches us that adversity shared with our Father, however, becomes a source of communion, courage, and hope.

YES

Hours before the trial that would lead to his death, Jesus lay face down, in numbing distress, in an olive grove on the outskirts of Jerusalem. Before him stretched two possible paths: one leading to safety, the other to a certain, terrible end. A few days before, Jesus had reminded himself of his mission. "Now my heart is troubled," he had said, "and what shall I say? 'Father, save me from this hour'? No, it was for this very reason [the cross] I came to this hour" (John 12:27).

Yet now, as the prospect of his suffering loomed immediately before him, Jesus revisited his options. "My soul is overwhelmed with sorrow to the point of death. . . . My Father, if it is possible, may this cup be taken from me" (Matthew 26:38, 39).

Jesus wondered, *Is it necessary? Are there no other options? Have I really understood the plan?* Ultimately, Jesus' struggle yielded this final place of rest: "If it is not possible for this cup to be taken away unless I drink it, may your will be done" (Matthew 26:42). Jesus said yes to his suffering.

In doing so, he embraced not primarily the suffering or even his mission, but his Father. "Not as I will, but as you will" (v. 39). Jesus' courage to say yes to suffering that at the moment, perhaps, he did not completely understand, sprang from the love and safety he felt in his relationship with his Father. Our ability to say yes to suffering, to embrace it, to drink our cup to the bottom, also is rooted in our trust of a Father we have gradually come to know as trustworthy and caring.

Jesus could say yes, too, because his suffering held no power over him as a statement of his worth. Later, as he hung unprotected on the cross, others interpreted his suffering as proof that Jesus was out of favor with God (Matthew 27:41-43). "We considered him stricken by God, smitten by him, and afflicted" (Isaiah 53:4). Suffering often brings with it questions about where we stand with God. Our urge to flee suffering is due not only to the pain it delivers but to a sensitive inner doubt it pricks. Henri Nouwen said, "Many people . . . don't think they are loved, or held safe, and so when suffering comes they see it as an affirmation of their worthlessness. The great question of ministry and the spiritual life is to learn to live our brokenness under the blessing and not the curse."[1]

Jesus lived his suffering under his Father's blessing—under his approval and affection. Jesus refused to see his trial as a sign of his Father's displeasure or disgust. This allowed him to rest and draw strength from his Father while suffering accomplished its work in him (Hebrews 5:8, 9).

Some of us are bearing suffering at this moment. We must

hold tight to our preciousness, our eternal belovedness, even in the jaws of the ordeal. Far from a comment on our worthlessness, suffering is the way to a richer experience of our sonship.

When our children were teenagers, they sighed and moaned at times when we intervened in their lives with correction and chastening. "Why can't you be like our friends' parents?" they asked. "They let their kids do whatever they want!" Now, as our children start having kids of their own, we are suddenly getting awards for caring enough to make them suffer certain inconveniences and disciplines when needed. "For the Lord corrects and disciplines everyone whom He loves, and He punishes, even scourges, every son whom He accepts and welcomes to His heart and cherishes" (Hebrews 12:6, *AB*).

"Shall trouble or hardship or persecution or famine or nakedness or danger or sword" (Romans 8:35) separate us from God's love? No! affirms the apostle Paul. Although many voices may try to convince us that our trials are proof that we have been abandoned, God says that "neither height nor depth, nor anything else in all creation, will be able to separate us from the love of God that is in Christ Jesus our Lord" (v. 39).

RIGHT HERE, RIGHT NOW

One morning some years ago, I was sitting at my office desk, minding my own business, when suddenly Gerri stood before me with a look on her face that, after twenty years of marriage, I recognized as meaning "Get ready for a stunner!" A moment later we pushed off into an eighteen-month trial that would test us on many levels. Gerri had just received a phone call from a customer of our small business that represented about half our income. The customer was closing its doors immediately. This came after news the week before that another customer, representing about 10 percent of our sales, was also shutting down. Suddenly, with two kids in college and me in seminary, we were down 60 percent. And the day was still young!

I recognized this trial. This smacked of a type God had offered, but I had manipulated my way out of, several times before. Now it had come knocking once again. I distinctly remember a moment in prayer the next day concerning this dilemma. Recognizing an opportunity to live some things with God that I had always fled in the past, I entreated him, "Lord, don't let me run. You know my habit, when faced with money problems, to panic and construct my own solutions. Please help me walk this one through with you. Lord (gulp!), I choose to be right here, right now, with you."

In Gethsemane, Jesus teaches us that we must choose our suffering. I don't mean that we can choose *whether* we will suffer. We will suffer. Suffering finds us. But even in the midst of afflictions that we cannot escape, we must embrace the experience, choose it, stop pining for other options. If we choose our suffering as Jesus did, for love of our Father, a brief inner death grows into a new, potent life with God.

If, on the other hand, we continually reject and flee our trials, we create an odd parallel life in which we try to live in our preferences rather than in the life we've been given. We become like people who refuse to go home as long as an unwelcome guest is there, who wander vagrantly through the streets in anger and unrest, suspended between two realities, never at home in either.

But we must go home. That's where our food waits, our bed, our shelter. "If it is not possible for this cup to be taken away unless I drink it, may your will be done" (Matthew 26:42).

Jesus also shows us that we must walk entirely through our suffering, avoiding the temptation to bail out. In his trial before Pontius Pilate, Jesus was repeatedly offered the opportunity to say a convenient word or two that would have had him back on the street in ten minutes (John 18:33-38; 19:5-12). But Jesus contented himself in his sufferings. "He was oppressed and afflicted, yet he did not open his mouth; he was led like a lamb to the slaughter, and as a sheep before her shearers is silent, so he did not open his mouth" (Isaiah 53:7).

Jesus, whose words had confounded his enemies on every occasion, now gave himself to silence. Oh, how I would love to have heard the conversation that passed between Jesus' heart and his Father's as he stood silent before Pilate. While his persecutors chattered like scolding monkeys, Jesus, for the joy set before him, embraced and re-embraced his suffering, throwing his heart continually up to God. Suffering must be willingly chosen, and once chosen, walked through to its end.

ANGELS SENT TO HELP US

Jesus' anguish in Gethsemane at one point became so intense that the Bible tells us "his sweat was like drops of blood falling to the ground" (Luke 22:44). In this distress "an angel from heaven appeared to him and strengthened him" (v. 43). Gethsemane shows us that we can expect comfort and inner resources to help us in our suffering.

To those undergoing trials, angels will be sent. But we must allow our angels to appear. It seems strange, but it is possible in suffering to be so busy protecting ourselves, to be so turned inward, so intent on our defenses, that no angel sent by God for our comfort can penetrate.

I have a friend who suffers back problems. The vertebrae of his lower back have shifted out of alignment, pinching nerves and causing nearly constant pain. The muscles in that area have become rock hard. The doctor said that the muscles, sensing something wrong, have formed a natural back cast to defend against the problem and protect the body from further damage.

In doing so, however, they have actually created worse problems, throwing the spine more seriously out of whack. The solution is to try, by various means, to get the muscles to relax and stop overprotecting the body. The doctor cannot even get at the real problem until he can get past the fortress of those muscles.

When suffering, try to hold your pain lightly, without too much self-protection. An inner posture of trust and release, an attitude that all will be well in God, gives our ministering angels—friends, family, Scripture, music, nature, tears, and even heavenly beings sent by God—a chance to appear, offering comfort and courage for our trial.

An Inner Magnificence

Back in that embarrassing decade called the seventies, I worked on a ministry team with a friend, Ed. Over time we got to know each other well. I liked Ed a lot. There was something about him, though, in those days, that always kept me in a low-level state of suspense. Ed suffered a lot of minor meltdowns in the ministry. Small trials could send him spiraling down into a pit of self-blame or rocket him into a hot criticism of others. Both problems, it seemed, sprang from impossibly high personal standards and a tense, legal relationship with God. Ed's rather unhappy life showed plainly in his face.

I had not seen Ed for nearly fifteen years when, by

chance, we met at a baseball game one day. As we caught up, I was immediately struck with a transformation in him. The tense edginess of former times had given way to a composed settledness and contentment that were remarkable and inspiring. I wanted to ask, "Ed, what happened?" I wondered whether I had just caught him on a good day or if this was the new Ed.

Several years passed before I saw Ed again. We had him over to the house for dinner and did a few things together while he was on furlough from the South American mission with which he has worked for many years. It turns out there had not been any single transforming event in Ed's life. His inner change, instead, resulted gradually from the practice of an important learned habit—a consistent, loving embrace of his Father in the long series of big and small trials committed to him along the road.

Traveling his own road, Jesus asked, "Did not the Christ have to suffer these things and then enter his glory?" (Luke 24:26). There is an expanding inner glory which is birthed through embracing trials, difficulties, and inconveniences for the love of God. This glory, I really think, is what I encountered in Ed. The faithful and patient embrace of his trials over many years had birthed a divine excellence, dignity, even magnificence— God's glory—in his soul.

The glory into which we enter through our suffering is not, of course, just the same as Jesus' glory. But it is made of the same stuff—the very weight and substance of God. "Now if we are children, then we are heirs—heirs of God and co-heirs with Christ, if indeed we share in his sufferings in order that we may also share in his glory. I consider that our present sufferings are not worth comparing with the glory that will be revealed in us" (Romans 8:17, 18).

But why suffering? How is God's glory birthed in us through trials and dilemmas in a manner it could not be without them? Is it not, perhaps, because afflictions attack the chief opponent to a relationship with God—our self-sufficiency? Suffering is not meant to distress us but to disable us. Suffering searches out the strong right arm that tries to solve life independently of God and inflicts on it a mortal wound, growing in its place a hand tightly clasped to the Father's.

We must become convinced of something that God has known for a very long time but we have not yet comprehended: "My grace is sufficient for you, for my power is made perfect in weakness" (2 Corinthians 12:9). The helplessness provoked by suffering gets us there. It creates in us a weakness that eventually convinces us to lay aside our innumerable fruitless strategies in exchange for God's unexpected solutions. "That is why," says Paul, "for Christ's sake, I delight in weaknesses, in insults, in hardships, in persecutions, in difficulties. For when I am weak, then I am strong" (v. 10).

BROKEN, GIVEN

My friend Ruth lost her husband to a sudden death four years ago. The years since have been a deeper and deeper resting in God's grace in the midst of her loss. Last week Ruth bumped into an old friend, Henry, at the grocery store. Henry's wife had recently died. Ruth's suffering became an instant bridge for Henry out of his numbing, isolating pain. Henry poured out his heart to another sufferer who could comfort him in his trouble with the comfort she herself had received from God. Jesus prepares our way for giving and receiving such comfort.

The Bible says, "Jesus took bread, gave thanks and broke it, and gave it to his disciples, saying, 'Take it; this is my body'" (Mark 14:22). Through his suffering, Jesus allowed himself to be broken and given, thereby becoming food for a hungry world. Only through his suffering did Jesus' impact burst beyond the confines of teacher and miracle worker to Savior. Our suffering, too, both breaks us and prepares us to be given as food for others. Through our mystical union with him, Jesus extends his nourishment, through us, his body, to a suffering world. "Praise be to the God and Father of our Lord Jesus Christ, the Father of compassion and the God of all comfort, who comforts us in all our troubles, so that we can comfort those in any trouble with the comfort we ourselves have received from God" (2 Corinthians 1:3, 4).

Shared pain strips away the veneer of pretense that dooms relationships to superficial levels, making us dare to reveal ourselves to one another. Jesus predicted, "I, when I am lifted up from the earth, will draw all men to myself" (John 12:32). Our cross—our suffering—is a partaking of his. As Jesus is perceived in us through our suffering, he draws and comforts others through us who are being led to intimacy by the same path.

OUR DANGEROUS ADVENTURE

The other night I got drawn into an old movie on TV. In it, a fellow jumped into the sea to save the life of a stranger. Safe once again on ship, the rescued man was dumbfounded that the other had risked his life to save him.

Gradually, amazement turned to devotion. Then as dilemmas began to mount, the man who risked his life was required to ask the man he saved to trust him in some dangerous risks. Each time the saved man swallowed hard, but figured, *This guy has proven himself to me. He's shown me his heart. I know he's on my side. I'll temporarily put aside my doubts and follow him.*

There is a certain emotional and rational logic to that story. Those who volunteer, under no compulsion, to undergo suffering on our behalf can be floated some grace during the odd moments when they ask us to follow them into suffering we don't understand. Jesus has earned our trust by entering—unasked—into our suffering.

[Jesus], being in very nature God,
  did not consider equality with God
  something to be grasped,
but made himself nothing,
  taking the very nature of a servant,
  being made in human likeness.
And being found in appearance as a man,
  he humbled himself
and became obedient to death—
  even death on a cross!
  —Philippians 2:6-8

God's intense concern for our well-being, proven in the incarnation and death of Jesus Christ, must be our focus when we face our cup of suffering. The man who jumped into the sea to save us may be trusted in every dangerous adventure into which he calls us to follow.

Further, we need to fix our attention on the end of the story. I have been a Christian for many years, but I find I still calculate my life in terms of the number of years I have left on earth. This planet, and my short span on it, the things I want to do, the health I want to maintain, the financial and other securities I want to achieve, are so very much my focus that any tiny fly in the ointment becomes a big, big deal. I wonder,

Am I willing to reassign my values? Am I willing to release my bear hug on this world and, at a deep level, switch my citizenship to Heaven? The day that I do, the trials and distresses God enlists to make me long for his eternal banquet will become dear friends rather than rude interruptions to my carefully protected agenda.

I feel challenged as I write this chapter. A voice calls, "Joel! Stop worriedly guarding a home that cannot last! I send you trials to convince you to build new foundations, not to defend old ones. When will you cast your eye beyond earth to Heaven? Begin to say good-bye. The clock is running down. Start to take your leave. Set your heart with me in paradise so that your sufferings may be servants, freeing your feet from the clinging earth." I remember Paul's words: "Since, then, you have been raised with Christ, set your hearts on things above, where Christ is seated at the right hand of God. Set your minds on things above, not on earthly things. For you died, and your life is now hidden with Christ in God" (Colossians 3:1-3).

In his sparkling little novel *The Great Divorce*, C. S. Lewis observes that for those journeying to Hell, the pleasures along the way will one day be seen to have been Hell all along, while for those journeying to Heaven the sufferings encountered will be seen to have been the stuff of paradise.[2] Lewis was in sync with this wisdom from Paul: "Therefore we do not lose heart. Though outwardly we are wasting away, yet inwardly we are being renewed day by day. For our light and momentary troubles are achieving for us an eternal glory that far outweighs them all" (2 Corinthians 4:16, 17).

Dear Jesus, is there a way the suffering I feel in my body and soul can become a meeting place for you and me? My pain often blooms so large it seems to push you from my world, leaving me to struggle alone. But I am not built to be alone with my distresses, Jesus. I'm not made to bear up under my affliction without a companion. Make my sufferings porous, Lord, so through them you can come to me. Make them a secret place where I can dwell with you, a fellow sufferer. In my grief, teach me to rest my spirit, as you rested yours, in our Father's care, the Father of mercies and God of all comfort.

Amen.

16 REST

"Daddy! Hold me!" Monica, our six-year-old, lifted herself into a teetering headstand by the coffee table.

"Daddy, be close! Catch me if I fall!" squealed our four-year-old, John, as he and David, our youngest, launched into a series of acrobatics across the carpet.

I barely noticed, however, as I plodded through the living room toward my home office on that mild fall evening many years ago.

"Daddy can't play tonight," said my wife, Gerri, quietly. "Daddy has to work."

"But he worked already," objected Monica.

"I know, honey," consoled Gerri, "but Daddy has to work some more."

Gerri was right. Daddy had to work some more. It seemed I could never work enough. My need to work had deep roots— religious ones. As I mentioned in an earlier chapter, growing up I somehow picked up the feeling about God that, although he loved me, he didn't like me very much. He loved me because he had to—he was God, after all—he was required to love me. But to get him to like me, to really approve of me, demanded that I turn in a perfect performance in everything I did. In every situation, I was supposed to be the hardest working, most earnest person in the room.

Now, that approach to life is pretty exhausting. As I sat down at my desk that night, I was a weary young man looking for a different way to live. But I also had a more immediate problem. Gerri and I were self-employed, and our small business was in trouble. Business had been bleak for months, and there did not appear any improvement on the horizon.

Night after night in my office, striving to fix my business problems, I could hear our children laughing and playing in the next room. It had been our longtime habit after supper to put on music and wrestle and dance. On this particular evening, I nearly wept, so badly did it hurt to neglect them. I wanted to hold them and goof around. I wanted to take them for a walk with their mom. I wanted to release this business problem and my whole wearisome life into God's hands. I desperately wanted to relax.

But I wouldn't let myself. I thought that would be irresponsible. It would show that I wasn't doing my best—and how could I earn God's mercy if I wasn't doing my best?

A couple of weeks later, brooding over these things, I was driving along a country road on a crisp afternoon when suddenly a massive flock of blackbirds rose from a field of autumn corn. Swirling dark and impressive against a brilliant blue sky, they were gathering in response to some inner signal, preparing to head south for the winter. As I watched and thought about my fearful, legal approach to life, I nearly shouted, "Why can't I be like those birds? Why can't I be free to do what my heart tells me and just trust God for the results?" At that instant, these verses from the Bible struck home: "Look at the birds of the air; they do not sow or reap or store away in barns, and yet your heavenly Father feeds them. Are you not much more valuable than they? Who of you by worrying can add a single hour to his life? . . . But seek first his kingdom and his righteousness, and all these things will be given to you as well" (Matthew 6:26, 27, 33).

Somehow, for the first time, I wondered, *What if that's true? What if God actually cares about me and has the power to help me? What if I'm allowed to relax, to rest, to trust in his love and mercy? What if it's OK to quit this never-ending struggle to perform for God and others, to justify my existence by what I produce?*

The novelty of these possibilities rattled around in me

over the next few days. Ultimately, I decided to take a chance. I determined to experiment with this new way of living. Instead of laboring alone over our business problems each night after dinner, I abandoned my office to spot cartwheels for my sons and practice headstands with my little girl. I took the kids on long evening walks for ice cream with their mom. I was not inactive in regard to our business, or nonchalant. I did the things I thought I should do but began to trust God to do the things only he could do.

As the months went by, God amazingly answered our business problems. But for me, that wasn't the real miracle. The deeper wonder was that I had tasted what it was like to relax a little. As I released my sense of obligation to construct my own solutions to life, something new was born inside me—something broad and spacious, simple and trusting, rooted in a profound acceptance of God's love for me. My many fears were replaced with a new confidence to launch into life calling to God, "Hold me, Daddy! Stay nearby. Catch me if I fall!"

THE TASTE OF REST

Every once in a while, we experience a pivotal moment in life that launches us in a new direction. My blackbirds epiphany was one of those for me. For someone who is by nature a Type A, whose inclination is always to be on task, and whose social and religious conditioning has been to find personal worth through the quantity and quality of what I produce, to taste the rest of God is a revelation.

Since that first taste, the undercurrent of my life has been to discover, more and more, how one lives in this new dimension. Words like *grace, rest, repose, abiding, leisure,* and *simplicity* have become friends. While the reasons for unrest in my life may be different than yours, it is likely that spiritual, emotional, and physical weariness find ways to make their presence known to you too.

This chapter continues the general themes of surrender and responsiveness we have been considering in previous chapters, looked at now from a slightly different perspective. Our key question: How does one release self-effort and striving, relaxing into a more leisurely, trusting, and grace-filled way of life?

GOOD AND POWERFUL

Our ability to rest is rooted in the goodness and power of God. The fact that God cares, and has the power to help us in our predicaments, makes it safe for the human heart to relax.

When I was ten or eleven years old, some friends of my parents asked me to babysit for the evening while they went dancing in a small town nearby. This couple, whom I did not know well, lived on a farm in the country. On returning from the dance about 1:30 AM, the husband, Tom, a big man, remote and silent, drove me home. Between their farm and our home lay a large, dark, uninhabited wood. The main road looped a long way around this wood, but through its middle twisted a shortcut rarely used—a narrow, rutted, waterlogged path barely wide enough for a single car. Suddenly, to my surprise, Tom nosed the car off the main road onto this forest track. As the dim headlights exposed the ghoulish shapes of leering trees, my imagination began to plague me about the man in the seat next to me. How well did I really know him? Why did he choose this way home? Why were we driving so terribly slowly through this awful wood? What did Tom have in mind? In a few minutes, we had slipped through the desolate wood, were back on the main road, and quickly in front of my home. I breathed a big sigh of relief, accepted my $1.75 for the evening, and went inside to bed.

What made my trip through the scary wood so very scary? Big Tom! Well, not poor Tom, really, but the fact that I did not know him. I did not know whether he was safe. I was unsure whether he cared about me. Had I been under the care of my dad or mom, I could have relaxed. I might even have fallen asleep. In fact, with someone who loved me and had the power to protect me, traveling through that deep forest in the middle of the night might even have seemed like a thrilling adventure. But I did not trust Tom. I was not convinced he was good. I didn't know for certain that he cared about me.

If, on our journey, we can once get our arms around the truth that the driver loves us, is in fact crazy about us, and is always on duty to provide for our deepest needs, we find we can start to relax during this ride through the dark and scary forest of life.

A key message of the Bible is this: God is good; he cares about me and is powerful to help me. "Can a mother forget the baby at her breast and have no compassion on the child she has borne? Though she may forget, I will not forget you! See, I have engraved you on the palms of my hands" (Isaiah 49:15, 16). Relaxing in Christ becomes the natural result of a deeper and deeper weaving of this reality throughout all the big and little needs, opportunities, questions, problems, and decisions of my life.

REST FROM, REST INTO

Because God is on our side and is constantly active to help us, we are privileged to rest from a wide variety of things that habitually harry the human race. In their place, God invites us to rest into an increasingly relaxed, expansive way of life. Following are nine key inward shifts that resting in Christ allows the human heart.

Rest from pretense into naturalness

One day at work, years ago, I realized I was behaving in a way that I didn't believe in just because an influential co-worker expected me to act that way. What was especially mystifying was that I had low respect for this person whom I was sacrificing my core self to please. The power of his personality simply swept over me, and I found myself acting a part that wasn't me.

Naturalness allows me to rest content in who I am. Pretense forms a picture of what I think I should be and prods me to play that role. But I need to ask: "Who wrote this role? Who created this part I feel so compelled to perform?" On reflection, I am likely to find that others wrote the role: co-workers, society, dissembling spirits, even people long dead (religious or cultural role models, even family ancestors).

For those who have become tired out by acting in someone else's play, the Bible offers this wonderful gift: "Do not think of yourself more highly than you ought, but rather think of yourself with sober judgment, in accordance with the measure of faith God has given you" (Romans 12:3). That is, discover your identity in Christ, release the demanding roles written by others, and rest naturally in who you are.

Rest from control into release

Try this little experiment. Stand on a busy street corner with your hands in your pocket and simply, by force of will, control the traffic as it goes by. Or look up in the sky and, by hard concentration, direct which way the clouds blow. Is it any less impossible to control the shifting details of your life?

The task of restraining, regulating, or managing the circumstances and people in our lives is exhausting. Why? *Because no grace has been assigned by God to support such work.* Grace lies elsewhere. "Come to me, all you who are weary and burdened," invites Jesus, "and I will give you rest. Take my yoke upon you and learn from me, for I am gentle and humble in heart, and you will find rest for your souls. For my yoke is easy and my burden is light" (Matthew 11:28-30). Rest does not result from corralling and taming the details of our lives but from exchanging their heavy yoke for Jesus' buoyant one. Because God is good and is always active to help us, we are invited to release the details of our lives to him, resting from the burden of control.

Rest from performance into grace

Many of us gratefully accept God's grace as our means of salvation, yet the idea of *living* by grace from moment to moment seems strange, almost irresponsible. Having accepted the gift of exchanging our own efforts to save our souls for simple trust in Jesus, we nevertheless spend our days working to justify our existence before God and others by the quantity and quality of what we produce. It is never enough. It is terribly exhausting.

One day, while jostling along a crowded street in the small Kentucky town near his monastery, Thomas Merton, the

Catholic monk and writer, was stopped in his tracks by a biblical truth suddenly made personal. How stunning, he realized, that through no effort or merit of our own, in Jesus Christ God opted to become one with ordinary human beings like those with whom Merton was bumping shoulders. He wrote in his journal, "To think that such a commonplace realization should suddenly seem like news that one holds the winning ticket in a cosmic sweepstake."[1]

What if we redeemed this cosmic sweepstake ticket, not only toward our eternal salvation but also toward daily living? What if our jobs, relationships, conversations, homes, and hobbies were lived under God's undeserved mercy? "At just the right time," says the Bible, "when we were still powerless, Christ died for the ungodly" (Romans 5:6). God's grace never flows to human achievement but to need. Consequently, we may rest from performing for God's approval and love and simply enjoy them each moment.

Rest from accumulation into contentment

The accumulation of money in this world, observes the main character in C. S. Lewis's novel *Perelandra*, is valued "chiefly as a defence against chance."[2] Guarding against the future in this way, however, can result in a wearying fixation on stocking and securing our personal larder. Francis de Sales, a spiritual mentor of the sixteenth century, paints a wonderful picture of our relationship with possessions as we journey through this world. We are to be like children "who with one hand hold fast to their father while with the other they gather strawberries or blackberries from the hedges. So too if you gather and handle the goods of this world with one hand, you must always hold fast with the other to your heavenly Father's hand and turn toward him from time to time to see if your actions or occupations are pleasing to him."[3]

In de Sales's scenario, the child's defense against an uncertain future is the security of the Father's hand. The apostle Paul gave words to this reality when he said, "I have learned the secret of being content in any and every situation, whether well fed or hungry, whether living in plenty or in want. I can do everything through him who gives me strength" (Philippians 4:12, 13).

Rest from regret into hope

Regret acts as a major drain of energy and joy in life. The vultures of regret search for the long-dead carcasses of personal disappointments and swirl around them, nipping, clawing, and jerking day and night at the remains. But Christians must bury their dead in Christ, trusting him to resurrect them to new life or let them lie, as he pleases. Lost opportunities, regretted actions, poor decisions—all must be released to die in

Christ so that they can also partake of his resurrection. What a wonderful thing to deliver our harassing, unsolvable regrets to God, allowing him to enfold them in his grace, thereby freeing us from their deathly grip. He can indeed restore the years the locusts have eaten! (See Joel 2:25.)

Rest from control into trust

On an icy winter morning, when I was six or seven years old, I pulled on my coat and boots and trudged down a gravel road to my friend's house, tugging a wooden sled behind me. When Jerry answered my knock, I uttered the magic words that unlocked the wonder of the next eight hours: "Wanna play?" From that moment, as we always did, we simply winged it. And had a fabulous day!

Children enjoy the wonderful freedom of not needing to know exactly what is going to happen next. Children follow their noses and simply trust that all will be well. Adults labor under a need to know precisely where every path is heading. Little nudges by God which, if heeded, would launch us on many grace-filled adventures, are often ignored because we can't see what is around the next bend. But for those who dare to become like children, God promises, "Whether you turn to the right or to the left, your ears will hear a voice behind you, saying, 'This is the way; walk in it'" (Isaiah 30:21).

To rest from control, the need for certainty, and to trust the journey is a renewing thing. Possibilities expand and miracles increase when the certainty police are allowed to go off duty.

Rest from judgment into mercy

In the 1980s film *Broadcast News*, the main character, Jane, is respected for her professional excellence but feared for her unremittingly high expectations of others. At a party, an annoyed co-worker snipes at Jane for her judging ways. "It must be nice," he jabs, "to always believe you know better—to always think you're the smartest person in the room." "No," Jane responds tiredly, "it's awful."[4]

It is an exhausting thing to sit in judgment of the world. Jesus invites us to release the burden of living our relationships in an attitude of critique, scrutiny, and correction.

"Do not judge, and you will not be judged. Do not condemn, and you will not be condemned. Forgive, and you will be forgiven" (Luke 6:37).

"Go and learn what this means: 'I desire mercy, not sacrifice.' For I have not come to call the righteous, but sinners" (Matthew 9:13).

Mercy and acceptance extended to others are joyful, broadening, and renewing. John Chrysostom, a Christian teacher of the fourth century, is said to have encouraged listeners, "Let us be inclined to show mercy and all other blessings will follow."

Rest from pride into humility

Some years ago, in a small group I attended, a wealthy and influential man in the corporate world shared that all his life what he really felt called by God to do was repair motorcycles. Years earlier, however, when the time had come to choose a career, he had not been comfortable imagining himself being introduced for the rest of his life as a motorcycle repairman. So, he chose an occupation that sounded more impressive. Now, twenty years later, though very successful, he regretted trading God's special call for one that better suited his pride.

Humility is a doorway into God's banquet hall. Humility helps us discern the aroma of nourishing foods from others that smell good for the moment but ultimately spoil, leaving us dissatisfied and drained. Humility salts our relationships, vocation, hobbies, and goals with the presence of Christ, of whom it declares, "He must become greater; I must become less" (John 3:30).

Rest from self into others

A pastor once put his finger on a fundamental anxiety that dogged his life. "I find I worry," he admitted to his congregation, "that if I give my life to serving others, who will take care of me?" The Bible acknowledges this concern and soothes it as it does all our worries: "Cast all your anxiety on him because he cares for you" (1 Peter 5:7).

God's care is constantly active on my behalf. The Bible says that God gives "to His beloved even in his sleep" (Psalm 127:2, *NASB*). Because my Lord is always on duty, looking out for my interests, I can rest from my preoccupation with protecting and serving myself and instead follow him into service of others.

A GOOD IDEA JUST IN TIME

There is a final, uniquely simple thing we can do to cultivate an experience of inner rest in our lives. It is a practice that is a little old-fashioned, somewhat out of favor, not especially trendy. It is hinted at in the following lines by Henry David Thoreau in his insightful essay "Life Without Principle":

This world is a place of business. What an infinite bustle! I am awaked almost every night by the panting of the locomotive. It interrupts my dreams. There is no sabbath. It would be glorious to see mankind at leisure for once. It is nothing but work, work, work. . . . If a man was tossed out of a window when an infant, and so made a cripple for life . . . it is regretted chiefly because he was thus incapacitated for—business![5]

Thoreau's words are humorous and oh so contemporary. They could have been written last week. Maybe it is because we are all so worn out that Thoreau's plea for a sabbath rest is beginning to make a comeback. I wonder if Thoreau realized that his heart expressed a hunger put there by the one who designed him. "Observe the Sabbath day by keeping it holy, as the LORD your God has commanded you. Six days you shall labor and do all your work, but the seventh day is a Sabbath to the LORD your God. On it you shall not do any work" (Deuteronomy 5:12-14).

Growing up in the 1960s, I tasted what it was like to have one day of the week more laid back, more given to worship, reflection, and relaxation. But an increasingly secular society decided it would be better to make every day just like every other. We thought, *Who wants to wait until Monday to buy a box of cornflakes when you can open the stores and get one on Sunday? Besides, it's good for the economy and a boon to the tax base.* We were further delighted to realize, *Hey! We've got more money and more urge to spend it these days, and here, right in front of our noses, is a whole extra day to do it!*

So gradually our ability to enjoy an important harbor of rest exited our lives. Now, however, many people are clamoring for a fresh taste of sabbath.

A sabbath is a time during the week when we unplug from the patterns that direct much of the rest of our lives. On our sabbath, we take a vacation from the musts, oughts, and shoulds that constantly beckon, exchanging them for a leisurely vacation for our souls. Sabbath rest oils our bruised joints and repairs our frayed ends. It relieves the emotional drain of constant problem solving and goal achieving, reducing our heartbeat back to healthy levels. Sabbath rest refills the cup from which we serve others. When we observe a sabbath, we are exercising active resistance against the modern tendency to spend our lives into the ground.

Sabbath, from the Hebrew *shabbat*, means "repose," or a cessation from exertion. Christian sabbath rest is an act of worship that takes part in the Spirit of God, who, after fruitful labor, also rested. "Thus the heavens and the earth were completed in all their vast array. By the seventh day God had finished the work he had been doing; so on the seventh day he rested from all his work. And God blessed the seventh day and made it holy, because on it he rested from all the work of creating that he had done" (Genesis 2:1-3).

Some of us, no matter what entertainment we engage in or diversions we employ, rarely experience a moment's true rest. One reason is hinted at in the adage "Wherever you go, there you are." One day a few years ago, Gerri and I went to a furniture store. As my eyes drifted over the rows of recliners, I stared, dreamy eyed, projecting the happy rest I would experience as the owner of a new chair. We bought a wonderful recliner and brought it home. Over the next months, although I sat in it often, I was puzzled that I rarely experienced the fulfillment of that blissful rest my longings had imagined. I finally realized the problem. Every time I sat down in the chair, I sat down with me! With my problems and projects and churning mental chores. Somehow, the luxurious fabric and cushy padding were overmatched by my own internal restlessness. But one of the most renewing things about the Sabbath is the permission it gives you to truly rest, to allow your mind to exit its mental racetrack in favor of a needed pit stop. I finally started to get my money's worth out of that chair when I discovered the Sabbath. The Sabbath put the rest into the recliner.

While Jesus was not legal in his observance of the Sabbath, he stated its significance positively when he said that "the Sabbath was made for man" (Mark 2:27; see vv. 23-28). This seems important. Jesus indicates that the one who built you has designed into you a need for regular pauses for physical, mental, and spiritual maintenance.

Let's briefly note three themes that help distinguish a sabbath from an ordinary day off: separation, communion, and renewal.

Separation

To his weary disciples Jesus said one day, "Come with me by yourselves to a quiet place and get some rest" (Mark 6:31).

The Sabbath calls us to come away from the things in life that draw down our reserves: the phone, the mall, the computer, wearying projects or problem solving, and more. Physical and mental separation from the things that deplete us is how sabbath rest begins.

Communion

Imbedded in Jesus' invitation above are three beautiful words: "Come with me." On our sabbath, we don't just go aside alone, but with him. This could take the form of some leisurely time with a book that stirs your soul or just the happy awareness that you are relaxing in him. On a recent sabbath, I napped on the couch for an hour or two, waking up at times to smile toward Heaven before slipping back into my dreams.

Renewal

More and more on my sabbath, I distinguish between entertaining activities that leave me keyed up inside versus restful ones that tend to refresh me. What activities do you find especially renewing? Reading, gardening, sports? Enjoy these as gifts during your sabbath.

It has sometimes been said, regarding the Sabbath, "Well, you know, since God is never concerned with outward observances but only our inward state, the practice of a literal sabbath is an idea whose time has long passed."

External activities, however, have an internal impact. A regular, literal sabbath allows an entry point of rest into your life. During World War II, the Allies were faced with conquering a Europe entirely under Axis occupation. They chose a thin strip of beach in France to serve as their launching point. From this small beachhead, they pushed their concentrated resources across France and into the heart of the Axis stronghold itself.

While I am not sure that war analogies are the very best way to communicate ideas about the Sabbath, still, there is a principle here. Capturing a day or part of a day each week as a regular sabbath has the effect of wafting rest and inner relaxation into the other days of our week as well. The habit of trust that the Sabbath helps us develop—trust to let go of our many pressing projects, to believe that life will wait while we pause and that God will hold everything safe in hand while we let go for a while—pushes beyond the borders of our sabbath time to season the rest of life as well.

Laps Are for Resting

About the time of my autumn revelation, shared earlier in this chapter, I received a second precious gift from God. Sitting alone in my home office one morning, I was reading a book.

Since I tend to be a morning person, it was quite early; no one else in the house was awake. Very quietly my office door opened and my son David, about three years old, walked into the room, just out of bed, eyes half closed, guided as if by radar to the only other person awake in the house. Without a word, David crawled onto my lap, snuggled around for a while, and became very still. Everything became still. And it was just one of those magic moments you get to experience every once in a while as a parent.

In a minute or two, David fell asleep. I thought, *Wow! Does it get any better than this? Just Dave and me.* At that moment, there was nowhere else on earth either of us would rather have been. I thought, *Don't leave, Dave. Don't remember that you got up to watch cartoons or eat Cheerios or anything else. Just stay here with me.*

Well, pretty soon David did remember why he had gotten out of bed in the first place, and he was gone. But in the few minutes we spent together, I learned something. It became abundantly clear to me what fathers both on earth and in Heaven desire. *Oh!* I thought. *I see! This is what my Father wants. He longs for me to put aside my busyness and many distractions and simply climb aboard him and relax in his company. He craves that moment when I want nothing more than him and he nothing more than me.*

While David rested in my lap, I did not scrutinize how he sat or lay. When he fell asleep, I didn't say "Now listen, son, if you truly valued our relationship, you'd prove it by being a little more attentive to me." No. I was delighted that I was the place that David chose to be so comfortable.

Ultimately, rest with God is a rest of relationship. It is a rest arising from God's desire to feel the seat of your pants upon his lap, the softness of your brow upon his breast. Rest arises and spreads itself through your life as, increasingly, you discover that you want nothing more than God, God nothing more than you.

Lord, this world is a hard taskmaster! It demands too much of me. I worry and work myself empty; still the world nips and pecks and is greedy for more. But lately I've caught the aroma of a new way to live. Is it true, Lord, that I can release my exhausting grip on the things that feel so threatening and relax my tired soul in you? Will you look out for me even if I am not constantly on duty, always at strained attention? Am I that precious to you that you would never forget about my needs? Lord, I am going to take a chance. I release now into your care this life I feel so responsible to guard and nurse and hold together. I release into your hand the things I so fret about and strive over but only you can do. Become my Sabbath, Lord. Become in me that inner rest I so long for and that is freely mine in you.

Amen.

17 RESPONSIVENESS

Early one October morning, some years ago, I sat at my desk pondering a stack of 350 stuffed and sealed envelopes awaiting a ride to the post office. These were invitations to six meetings in our home scheduled to begin three weeks from that day. During these gatherings, my wife and I would lay out to friends and relatives our plans for a new ministry: WellSpring Life Resources. At the thought of these meetings, suddenly, for the very first time, after years of planning and anticipation, I got cold feet.

Seven years earlier, responding to a growing call of God, I had embarked on a path that would lead me out of the business world into the very ministry we were ready to announce. It took a long time to get the ship turned around. First, I had to finish my college work (which I had been too smart to bother with earlier in life), then attend evening seminary while working full-time in the small business my wife and I operated. It was an exhausting yet exhilarating time.

While in seminary, I spent literally hundreds of hours in prayer regarding the mission of this new ministry. By the time I sat staring at that pile of signed invitations, I had developed core ministry values, mission statements, and goals. I had formed a board of directors and written curriculum and ways to promote it. I had things worked up, tied down, and ready to rip. And now—second thoughts.

My problem, I think, had to do with the way I am wired. Being a private person, I don't naturally enjoy the spotlight. The mental picture of dumping all those invitations into the mail and from that moment forward being publicly on record as going ahead with this ministry—scrutinized regarding fund-raising, curriculum, timetables, goals, and motives—made me shiver. The heart of the ministry—the retreats, classes, groups, and workshops—excited me. But now, the thought of all the little attendant uncertainties and concerns began to press in.

Would anyone be interested? Would Gerri and I retain our identity apart from the ministry? What if we couldn't sell our small business and, after announcing a start to the ministry, we had to delay it indefinitely? And what about our friends? Would our relationships change? Would they think we were after their money? Would they smile kindly but secretly think we were nuts to have launched out on this ministry caper?

As long as God's call had been somewhere out there in the future, it felt like an adventure. Now that it was in my face, it just felt threatening. I began to reason. *You know, I wonder if I am not rushing things a bit. Maybe it would be better to wait another year, become a little more financially secure, get our organizational structure absolutely in place.* All at once a more relaxed schedule sounded awfully good. Deep inside I knew the way forward (we often do, don't we?), but the uncertainties of my situation made responding to God's guidance suddenly seem unrealistic, impractical, dangerous.

Do you connect with the tug-of-war that was going on inside me? Guess what? Everybody does! The apostle Paul did (see Romans 7). His friend Peter did (see Galatians 2). All of us who journey forward with God feel pushed and pulled to delay responding to his call by circumstances that seem a bit too pressing—to put God and convictions aside for just a little while until we get through this one tight spot. We don't feel proud of our compromises, but sometimes the consequences of obedience look so disagreeable that we feel we have no other option.

In recent chapters, we have been considering a lifestyle marked by a growing spirit of surrender and responsiveness to God in all of our activities. But if you are like most people, as you surrender your heart to God, it's not long before you become amazed at what an unpredictable heart it is! Long habits of self-protection don't give way easily to trusting responsiveness to God. Jesus may be our chosen master, but he has a long way to go to win all of our affection.

This final chapter of the book ponders the future, asking, "As I move forward on my journey, how will Jesus Christ and his call become the options in life that my heart habitually prefers? How will this new thing that I've started to taste in Christ reach inside and lay hold of my deepest parts? How will the Already dimension of life that we have been speaking of throughout this book—that renewed, countercultural way of living that rises up out of the cross and resurrection of Jesus—become the personal trademark of my soul?"

Unlike the choice to surrender individual situations to God, which may be decided in the space of a moment, this deep, organic exchange of natures is a gradual process that takes place, step by step, over a lifetime. But our destination is definite. For the Christian, the eventual re-creation of our inner being is the sure result of the journey on which we've embarked. The new country we have entered never had it in mind to simply waft us a few comforting breezes or provide us a place to vacation from our regular world. It wants to *become* our regular world. It wants to become, in fact, a new world inside us, remaking all our inner geography. Its message to the Christian traveler is "Those who enter here may not keep their old mountains and valleys and oceans and streams. Here, a whole new landscape must grow up inside of you."

It's not as though you have no choice in this, of course. But as the old saint told the seeker who decided that Christianity demanded too much, "Of course, it's up to you. You may turn away whenever you want. But there is nowhere else to go."

For those who desire to walk this journey forward into increasing fullness, who are willing to embrace the thrills and chills of continual inner reconstruction, who recognize a tendency within to flee but a corresponding pull to respond to God, how do we move ahead? In one of those interesting ironies that seem to abound in the spiritual life, responsiveness to God is both our challenge *and* our path forward.

THE RESPONSE THAT TRANSFORMS

Have you ever fallen asleep in a public place and amused the people around you by waking up with a jerk as you tried to fend off some threatened dream-danger? I've treated people to this special entertainment in schools, churches, shopping malls, and other public places over the years. Human beings have an absolutely instinctive tendency to protect themselves from things that threaten.

I used to play a game with my kids in which I would quickly pass my open hand in front of their eyes. If they could resist blinking, I'd give them a nickel. It used to break me up to watch their determined little faces, eyes bugging out, trying hard not to blink. But I didn't lose many nickels. That reliable, built-in defense mechanism that protects the eye when things get too close always kicked in—whether my kids wanted it to or not.

Humans have a deep psychological tendency to protect themselves. Most turn inward and power up their defenses at the first sign of danger. It is this innate tendency to self-protect that seems to be at the heart of most Christian unresponsiveness to God. Christians normally don't disobey God because they love sin. Usually, unresponsiveness is rooted in fear—a fear that what God is asking will somehow be too much to handle—mentally, emotionally, or physically. When the threat becomes too much to bear, we dive for cover.

Personally, although I have surrendered my heart in both general and specific instances to God many times over the years, I still notice a quivering tendency to avoid God's solutions to life when they appear too threatening. This tendency is so natural, in fact, that it is unconscious. I do it without trying. I do it without knowing. I do it all the time. This fact puzzles me because I know I love God. I know I want him. I am thrilled at his presence in my life. But still, there it is.

The story of Moses in the Old Testament holds much help for resolving this perplexing contradiction. Unlike some Bible characters whose lives Scripture only dips in and out of rather quickly, in Moses we are allowed to observe the full arc of one man's deepening, transforming relationship with God. Let's spend some time with Moses, allowing him to share his hard-earned lessons toward developing a life increasingly responsive to God.

REVOLT OR RESPOND

Early on in Exodus 3, Moses' very first private audience with God is going very well: "The LORD said, 'I have indeed seen the misery of my people in Egypt. I have heard them crying out because of their slave drivers, and I am concerned about their suffering. So I have come down to rescue them from the hand of the Egyptians and to bring them up out of that land into a good and spacious land, a land flowing with milk and honey'" (vv. 7, 8).

Hey, this is starting fine! The rescue of his relatives is welcome news, and Moses is impressed and attentive. But suddenly the other shoe drops as God shocks this quiet, elderly sheepherder from Midian with a stunning assignment: "So now, go. I am sending you to Pharaoh to bring my people the Israelites out of Egypt" (v. 10).

What? Talk about a U-turn! A delightful vision of God just went south awfully fast. Moses is to go to Egypt to free the Israelites from the ruthless taskmasters for whom they have served as a favorite source of slave labor for hundreds of years! When Moses recovers his voice, he wastes no time informing God that this is an assignment he wants no part of. And thus begins a tense negotiation in the Sinai desert that no doubt every angel in the area not on another assignment fluttered intently forward to enjoy.

But Moses said to God, "Who am I, that I should go to Pharaoh and bring the Israelites out of Egypt?"

And God said, "I will be with you. And this will be the sign to you that it is I who have sent you: When you have brought the people out of Egypt, you will worship God on this mountain."

Moses said to God, "Suppose I go to the Israelites and say to them, 'The God of your fathers has sent me to you,' and they ask me, 'What is his name?' Then what shall I tell them?"

God said to Moses, "I AM WHO I AM. This is what you are to say to the Israelites: 'I AM has sent me to you.' . . .

"But I know that the king of Egypt will not let you go unless a mighty hand compels him. So I will stretch out my hand and strike the Egyptians with all the wonders that I will perform among them. After that, he will let you go." . . .

Moses answered, "What if they do not believe me or listen to me and say, 'The LORD did not appear to you'?" (Exodus 3:11-14, 19; 4:1).

And now, to encourage Moses that he could be counted on to support him in this difficult assignment, God performed a series of miracles and gave Moses the power to do the same. Still Moses groped for the back door:

Moses said to the LORD, "O Lord, I have never been eloquent, neither in the past nor since you have spoken to your servant. I am slow of speech and tongue."

The LORD said to him, "Who gave man his mouth? Who makes him deaf or mute? Who gives him sight or makes him blind? Is it not I, the LORD? Now go; I will help you speak and will teach you what to say."

But Moses said, "O Lord, please send someone else to do it."

Then the LORD's anger burned against Moses (Exodus 4:10-14).

Hmmm. As a reader, I begin the account by identifying with Moses. After all, this is a huge task. Moses feels inadequate, unprepared. My own objections would be about the same. Who can blame him for not wanting to go?

But as God patiently (and miraculously) answers one objection after another, I begin to become uncomfortable. Moses simply won't put away his excuses. I want to whisper, "Moses, this is Yahweh you're arguing with. He can squash you like a bug. Do what he tells you!"

But Moses plows on. "Oh no, Lord. Don't send me! They won't listen. They won't believe me. They don't know me. I'm not eloquent. Surely this won't work. Oh, please send someone else!" Finally, verse 14 erupts with the alarming line, "Then the LORD's anger burned against Moses."

Ouch!

Why did Moses so desperately want out of this assignment? Why didn't he want to go? What was going on inside him to make him look so feverishly for an exit from this task? Was it because Moses didn't want his relatives, the Israelites, to be free? Was it because he loved his life tending his father-in-law's sheep so much that he could not bear the thought of doing something else for a living? Not likely. The real reason, hinted at by Moses himself, contains a key to helping us understand God's goal in asking Moses, and us, to obey: "Who am I, that I should go to

Pharaoh and bring the Israelites out of Egypt?" (Exodus 3:11).

Let's reflect. Until this moment in his life, Moses had not seen God act in impossible situations. So, like us, Moses measured God's calling to him against his own abilities and concluded not only that there was no chance for success but also that he probably would not survive the adventure. "Who am I that God thinks I can go to Pharaoh and convince him to let these people go? That's outrageous!"

Have you ever noticed, like Moses, that when it comes to God's call, he often asks you to do things that you absolutely cannot do? Not only does he ask you to do things you don't want to do (that's hard enough), he also asks you to do things that are truly beyond your ability to accomplish. It seems almost cruel. Why does he do that?

Why does God confront Moses with the impossible assignment of forcing a tyrant ruler to give up his country's best source of slave labor? Why does he make Moses a deliverer to this group of people who largely just want to be left alone? And further, later in the account, when Moses has finally agreed to obey and is faithfully doing his best to accomplish the work, why does God seem to sabotage Moses' efforts by allowing problem after problem to trip him up and slow him down?

When God seems to be acting in a contradictory manner, there is usually something he's trying to accomplish that demands the contradiction. That's the case here. Moses himself reveals God's strategy later in the story, when he finds himself in the middle of another in a series of impossible jams. Blocked by the Red Sea on one side and an attacking Egyptian army on the other, Moses (now starting to get into the groove of God's program) shouts to the Israelites this electric command: "Stand firm and you will see the deliverance the LORD will bring you today" (Exodus 14:13).

"Stand firm and you will see the deliverance the Lord will bring!" That is God's reason for obedience. That is the fruit of responsiveness. That is why he pushes you beyond your abilities, backs you into situations with no natural solution, and calls you to do things you cannot naturally do. There is a quality of life God wants to show you, those around you, and a watching world that he cannot—he need not—as long as you remain able to handle every situation yourself.

So God pushes us into corners. He erects huge walls before us. He hems us in and squeezes away our options until there is nothing left for us to do but flee or trust. Mutiny or obey. Revolt or rely on him. If we risk responding, we find ourselves taking part in God's supernatural solution to our dilemma. And here is the key: as we become caught up in the swirl of this activity, we become changed. It is as though in the process of transforming the situation, God's miracle filters through us, transforming us as well!

We begin to look at the world in a different way. We "catch" some of God. Our appetite for him increases. Our dread of his call diminishes. Before, when we heard his voice, we trembled and wondered, *Oh no! Now what?* But now a strange thing starts to happen. We find that God's voice begins to thrill us, to remind us of past miracles, to open our eyes to future possibilities. Inside there is a new person being formed, one a little more daring, a little more trusting. Our heart for God is expanding. The concerns that used to keep us from responding to him begin to look quite puny against the new quality of life we've started to experience.

This change doesn't happen all at once, but slowly, over time. The Bible shows an early Moses who was allergic to obedience. Every time Moses spoke, in the early days, it seemed he was objecting in some way or other to what God was asking of him. Even after he began to obey God, Moses had regular relapses when he wished this whole new way of life would just go away (see Exodus 5:22, 23).

As he went on, however, Moses saw God work. He developed a personal history with God and began to gain his perspective. Slowly but surely, he acquired a taste for God's methods over his own. It became a habit, then a passion. Time and again, Moses let God invade his life through obedience. Each time God worked two separate miracles: he changed the situation, and he changed Moses.

After forty years of such interaction with God, it was said of Moses at the time of his death, "No prophet has risen in Israel like Moses, whom the LORD knew face to face, who did all those miraculous signs and wonders the LORD sent him to do in Egypt—to Pharaoh and to all his officials and to his whole land. For no one has ever shown the mighty power or performed the awesome deeds that Moses did in the sight of all Israel" (Deuteronomy 34:10-12).

What happened to the original Moses, the hand-wringing excuse factory of Exodus 3 and 4? This later Moses is a different fellow. Changed. Converted. Convinced. By constantly putting himself in the place where God was working, Moses himself was transformed into something new.

So the beautiful gift of responsiveness to God is its tendency to draw us within the circle of God's activity. Once there, the power of God's Spirit touches us in our ready places, and we slowly, but very surely, become new people.

HOLDING TO THE ROAD

In Minnesota we are proud of our blizzards. Blizzards prove what we have suspected all along—that we are remarkable people, durable, somehow more substantial than those who spend too much time in the sun. A television commercial runs here every winter featuring a Minnesotan pushing his way through an incredible blizzard to get to a favorite retailer. This fellow, head down, resolute, struggling bravely forward in defiance of the elements, is a picture to me of what responding to God sometimes feels like, especially in its early moments—sheer will, an inch at a time, often accompanied by thoughts like *How on earth is God going to get me through this? Any minute now I'm going to hit the wall. Can this really be God's will for me? Oh Mama—I'm too young to die!*

Responding to God's call does not always feel good. Teresa of Avila, a sixteenth-century Christian teacher, is said to have once complained to God about the difficulties of a certain road he was asking her to walk. God's response was simple. "But Teresa," he said, "this is how I treat all my friends." To which Teresa replied, "Then I see, Lord, why you have so few of them!"

Moses may have wondered, too, how many friends God had. God's commands to Moses were absolute stunners. And, generally, God did not offer a Plan B. When God wanted something done, he had in mind a specific thing, and there it was, take it or leave it. Embrace it or flee. Respond or disobey.

And this brings us to one more lesson Moses has to teach us about responding to God.

A FULL IMPRESSION

After working hard to escape God's call early on, Moses eventually agreed to go. He still had no idea how he would accomplish the task. The same fears that assaulted him on the mountain of the burning bush continued to hound him into Egypt. For a long time, he stayed unconvinced about this whole deliverance idea. But the key thing is this: He went. He did it. He responded. He did not flee.

In the end, this is Moses' most important lesson to us: *he didn't flee.* Though at the beginning he was not quite a model of trusting responsiveness, he did the main thing—he went. I have stood shuddering on the road of obedience many times, half expecting at any moment to be squashed out of existence by the problems ahead. But in staying on the road, walking forward, gripping his hand, refusing to leave the path down which God calls me, God has time and again worked miracles that have changed the situation I faced and changed me.

Remember my intense reluctance, at a critical moment, to follow through with God in the launching of my new ministry? At just the moment I was to mail the announcements of WellSpring's startup to everybody I knew, I was deep in second and third thoughts. Though my own assignment was not at the level of an Egyptian deliverance, it was big enough for me. And it threatened enough unpleasant possibilities to make me suddenly nostalgic for safer days. I thought, *I love you, Lord, but I'd sure love to ease back on the throttle a little!*

In this wavering state of mind, I picked up my Bible for a

daily time of meditation and prayer. The passage for the day happened to be this:

> Jesus replied, "The hour has come for the Son of Man to be glorified. I tell you the truth, unless a kernel of wheat falls to the ground and dies, it remains only a single seed. But if it dies, it produces many seeds. The man who loves his life will lose it, while the man who hates his life in this world will keep it for eternal life. Whoever serves me must follow me; and where I am, my servant also will be. My Father will honor the one who serves me.
>
> "Now my heart is troubled, and what shall I say? 'Father, save me from this hour'? No, it was for this very reason I came to this hour. Father, glorify your name!" (John 12:23-28).

Wow! God galvanized my attention with those words. They both challenged and comforted me. I felt deeply appreciative that God would so kindly acknowledge my fears and encourage me forward. While a moment earlier my attention had been on all the threatening uncertainties that lay ahead, now my focus went to the assurance of his company in the adventure. I took a deep breath, dropped the envelopes in the mail, and welcomed the future.

As I have learned lessons of obedience like this over the years, God has slowly worked in me as in Moses. Bumping up against the power of God, regularly turned loose in my life through faith and obedience, I am slowly but surely becoming a new person.

These days, I am more willing to trust him, to take him at his word. I find I get charged up by comments like those of George Mueller, the wonderful man of faith of the nineteenth century, who took a secret delight when things looked their bleakest because it was then that he knew that God was about to do what only he could do.[1]

There are times yet during difficult moments when I am tempted to help God along, times when he seems to move too slowly or goes in a direction I do not understand. But the hundreds of times I have been drawn in as he powerfully swirled through the dilemmas of my life have changed me for good. They have planted my convictions deeper, made my faith more real, and progressively won my reluctant heart for God.

I had a professor of Old Testament years ago, a Chinese man by the name of Dr. Wong, new to our country, still learning the language. His depth in God was rivaled only by his difficulty in being understood by his students. But it was always worth listening closely. One day, in a little aside that perhaps all my classmates promptly forgot, Dr. Wong gave me a lasting picture of the effect of obedient responsiveness to God on the soul. Dr. Wong said (insert heavy Chinese accent), "We are like de piece of hard rubber. When we obey God, it make dent on our heart. This dent slowly go away, leaving only small impression. When we obey again, dent go deeper, then go away a little, leaving deeper impression. Each time we obey, dent go deeper—until very deep!"

Thank you, Dr. Wong.

The Nourishing Way

So your life, like mine, is in process. We are like the hard rubber. In the years ahead, we may expect God to allow us a steady diet of challenging situations surrounded by his caring and miraculous availability. These are offered to encourage us toward the fruitful way, the nourishing way, the way of responsiveness.

As we respond to the Spirit's calling, however imperfectly, in the many ways we have explored throughout this book— through Scripture and prayer, in our special purpose and calling, in his invitation to embrace surrender, rest, redemptive suffering, and more—we are increasingly transformed in Christ. Responsiveness to the Holy Spirit is the narrow gate through which all who desire may step into the loving, intimate, and transforming experience of God our hungry hearts so crave.

I'm so glad we got to enjoy this banquet together. It's an honor to join you at our rich, common table. Though we may never meet, our hearts beat along similar lines. We share the pain of our incompleteness yet also the certain hope of our completion in Christ.

Encourage all you can to draw their chairs up to this feast. People are hungry and weary and so in need of lasting nourishment. Together, let's live to help famished lives find their way to Jesus Christ, the heart's food and drink, the craving of our souls.

I pray that out of his glorious riches he may strengthen you with power through his Spirit in your inner being, so that Christ may dwell in your hearts through faith. And I pray that you, being rooted and established in love, may have power, together with all the saints, to grasp how wide and long and high and deep is the love of Christ, and to know this love that surpasses knowledge— that you may be filled to the measure of all the fullness of God (Ephesians 3:16-19).

Amen.

Dear Father, reading this book has shown me that everything you are and do calls for a responsive heart in me. Your goodness and power invite me to restful trust. Your nourishing Word directs me to healthy paths. Your holiness and intimacy stir me to awed worship. Your purpose for my life invites me to courageous adventure. There is nothing on earth that calls so deeply or is so worthy of my total response. Only you can return my feeble yes with the power, nourishment, and well-being for which a human soul hungers. Only you, dear Father, you my Jesus, you our Holy Spirit are mercy, wisdom, glory, joy, and strength. To you my heart responds, my soul clamors, and my life is poured out today, tomorrow, and forever and ever!

Amen and amen!

NOTES

CHAPTER 3, ALREADY, NOT YET

1. Brent Curtis and John Eldredge, *The Sacred Romance* (Nashville, TN: Thomas Nelson, Inc., 1997), 172.

2. Thomas Merton, *The Ascent to Truth* (New York: The Viking Press, 1959), 24.

CHAPTER 4, LIBERTY

1. Jeanne Guyon, *Experiencing the Depths of Jesus Christ* (Sargent, GA: Christian Books Publishing House, 1975), 7.

2. Ibid., 8.

CHAPTER 6, UNSTUCK

1. Ralph Gower, *The New Manners & Customs of Bible Times* (Chicago: Moody Press, 2005).

CHAPTER 7, TRANSPARENCY

1. Blaise Pascal, translated by W. F. Trotter, *Pensées*, (Chicago: The University of Chicago, 1952), 222.

2. Etty Hillesum, translated by Arnold J. Pomerans, *Etty Hillesum: An Interrupted Life* and *Letters from Westerbork* (New York: Henry Holt and Company, 1996), 345.

CHAPTER 8, LISTENING

1. George MacDonald, *The Elect Lady* (Fairfield, IA: 1st World Library—Literary Society, 2004), 64, www.1stworldlibrary.org

CHAPTER 9, WORSHIP

1. A. W. Tozer, *The Pursuit of God* (Camp Hill, PA: Christian Publications, Inc., 1993), 36, 41.

CHAPTER 10, PURPOSE

1. Oswald Chambers, edited by Jim Reimann, *My Utmost for His Highest* (Grand Rapids, MI: Discovery House Publishers, 1992), January 2.

CHAPTER 11, CALLING

1. George Mueller, compiled by A. E. C. Brooks, *Answers to Prayer* (Chicago: Moody Press), 6.

2. J. C. Pilkington, translator, *The Confessions of St. Augustine* (Cleveland: Fine Editions Press), 36, 37.

CHAPTER 12, SELF-DISCOVERY

1. Others hold that the designation *apostle* should only be given to those who both exhibit these characteristics and had also personally been with the risen Christ. Paul is included in this group through his encounter with Christ by a special vision (Acts 9:1-8).

2. While not evident in the New Testament lists of gifts, this special ability fostering worship of God evidences itself in the Old Testament (e.g. Exodus 28:1-3; 31:1-11; I Kings 7:13-45) and in the church throughout its history to the present day.

CHAPTER 13, TRANSFORMATION

1. Frederick Buechner, *Godric* (New York: HarperSanFrancisco, 1980), 120.

CHAPTER 14, SURRENDER

1. T. A. Hegre, *The Cross and Sanctification* (Minneapolis, MN: Bethany Fellowship, Inc., 1960).

CHAPTER 15, SUFFERING

1. Henri Nouwen, interview quoted in "Deepening Our Conversation with God," *Leadership* (Winter 1997, Vol. 28, No. 1), 112, http://www.ctlibrary.com/le/1997/winter/71112a.html

2. C. S. Lewis, *The Great Divorce* (New York: MacMillan Publishing Company, 1946), 67-68.

CHAPTER 16, REST

1. Thomas Merton, edited by Lawrence S. Cunningham, *Thomas Merton: Spiritual Master* (Mahwah, NJ: Paulist Press, 1992), 145.

2. C. S. Lewis, *Perelandra* (New York: Simon & Schuster, 1996), 48.

3. St. Francis de Sales, translated by John K. Ryan, *Introduction to the Devout Life* (New York: Doubleday, 2003), 141.

4. *Broadcast News*, directed by James L. Brooks, Twentieth Century Fox Corporation, 1997.

5. Henry David Thoreau, *Civil Disobedience* (Amherst, NY: Prometheus Books, 1998), 64-65.

CHAPTER 17, RESPONSIVENESS

1. Basil Miller, *George Mueller: Man of Faith & Miracles* (Minneapolis, MN: Bethany Fellowship, Inc., 1941), 62.

STUDY GUIDES

The *Soul Craving Group Member Discussion Guide,* a six-session small group or classroom study, is available from Standard Publishing (ISBN 978-0-7847-1993-0). Visit www.standardpub.com or call 1-800-543-1301.

❧

WellSpring Life Resources offers thirteen- and eighteen-session *Soul Craving* study guides, in addition to a variety of other curriculum materials.

For more information, to order materials, or to learn about the author's availability for retreats, classes, workshops, and conferences, please contact WellSpring Life Resources:

- on the Web: www.WellSpringLifeResources.com
- by phone: 1-888-604-0373
- or by e-mail: info@WellSpringLifeResources.com